Editors assistants: Lucile Arnaud, Simon Duhamel

Special Thanks to:
Jean Bréhat
Rachid Bouchareb
Muriel Merlin
Delphine Coualan
Julie Poissier
Alban Barré
Stephan May

Ouvrage publié avec l'aide du
Ministère français chargé de la Culture

© Éditions Dis Voir, 2001
3, rue Beautreillis
75004 Paris
ISBN 2-914563-03-5

© photos Bruno Dumont

PRINTED IN EUROPE

All right reserved. No part of this publication may be reproduced, adapted or translated in any country. Intellectual property laws forbid making copies or reproductions destined for collective use. Any reproduction in whole or in part by any means whatsoever without the express consent of the author or his agent is unauthorised and constitutes an infringement of Articles 425 and following of the Code.

BRUNO DUMONT

this series edited by
DANIÈLE RIVIÈRE

in the same serie

TSAI MING LIANG
Olivier Joyard
Jean-Pierre Rehm
Danièle Rivière

WONG KAR WAI
Jean-Marc Lalanne
David Martinez
Ackbar Abbas
Jimmy Ngai

ATOM EGOYAN
Carole Desbarats
Jacinto Lageira
Danièle Rivière
Paul Virilio

PETER GREENAWAY
Daniel Caux
Michel Field
Florence de Mèredieu
Philippe Pilard
Michael Nyman

RAOUL RUIZ
Christine Buci-Glucksmann
Fabrice Revault D'Allonnes

MANOEL DE OLIVEIRA
Yann Lardeau
Philippe Tancelin
Jacques Parsi

BRUNO DUMONT

SÉBASTIEN ORS

PHILIPPE TANCELIN

VALÉRIE JOUVE

1 ▶

2 ▶

BRUNO DUMONT	11	**THE WORK OF A FILMMAKER** Translated by J. Ames Hodges
SÉBASTIEN ORS	23	**POETICS OF FATALITY** Translated by Paul Buck & Catherine Petit
PHILIPPE TANCELIN	39	**ENQUIRIES ON REALITY** Translated by J. Ames Hodges
VALÉRIE JOUVE	105	**DIALOGUE IN SPACE AND TIME** Translated by J. Ames Hodges
	122	**BIOGRAPHY**
	123	**FILMOGRAPHY**
	127	**PHOTO INDEX**

The end [1]

(sequence 1)

All my food was coming back up, at the wheel, down my chest, while my colleagues were still cursing about the horror spread out before them: the dismembered parts had been scattered on the ground, just past the car in the rocks, the Joshua trees, the dust and the bitterness of the desert. Paul came to the car door and crouched down next to me without even a word about the remains. He asked if I was feeling okay and I stared at him wildly, sapped by all the blood. He took off, preferring the others; I started driving away along the road.

I was soaked and disgusting, abject, and my own stench forced me to get out, a little farther along, less than a kilometer away, to tear off the top half of my duds and be alone, then, with my shock in the middle of the Chollas.

THE WORK OF A FILMMAKER

Summer 2000, scouting for *The end*, I steal a dead trunk from the Joshua Tree desert in California.

Am preparing a feature-length film.

Took months to write it alone. Hour after hour in front of the screen waiting for it to come: writing slowly, adjourning…

Everything must come from drawing. Giacometti.

Am a *writer* first – modest and temporary – concerned with expression, through words, states (of being and of landscapes). Invent a story where individuals meet. Banal or indifferent plot, unimportant; only its movement counts so that the characters interact and reveal themselves.

Always write there from the only angle and hope of literature and not cinema. Am completely for the expression of an art that excludes all the others. Cinema has nothing to do with and nothing of writing, it is a distinct art.

(I never try to film what I write, because it can't be filmed.)

I do not adapt anything. I expect nothing.

I have settled on writing – for the time being – to express, in this way, a statement. Then I get rid of it. I regress and stay quiet: the beginning of cinema.

I free myself from words, even dialogues. (Hearing or seeing on screen something that has been written is no longer tolerable.)

Cinema is another matter and does not follow from writing: It is writing. The filmmaker stays quiet, works in the silence that comes before the writer. Mute.

He is wild. He goes where everything begins, life itself, its substance. This is cinema's capacity to be a *primal* art; it can end where literature begins, being and limiting itself to representing the very substance of our lives, in other words, to our bodies, to incarnation.

The body is the beginning of the soul, the primal matter and the substance of filmmaking.

---

1) The end, Bruno Dumont's upcoming film now in preparation (see p. 9 a passage from the screenplay-sequence 1). The pictures taken during his wanderings in the Californian desert and that circulate throughout the book come from his scouting work for the film. (Editor's Note)

The senses are the cause of concepts, the body is the cause of the soul and precedes it in the intellect. Philoxenos of Mabourg.

Cinema is *metaphysical*. It resides in the foundations and principles of the human condition, worldly existence.

So I film the beginning of beings, their start: I film bodies, living, active, drawn to, repulsed from each other. I am in their faces. Limit myself to filming the corporeal, the visible.

I film the earth and trees, the wind. Faces.

(At length, the invisible appears. The invisible cannot be filmed.)

Cinematography is inhuman. It comes before the other arts: it is the very beginning of the world, the substance of our lives. It is inhuman because it goes to the edge of the condition. It is in the expression of our first endeavors, the movements of our lives. It is life itself, presented and represented.

So there you have, perhaps, cinema and its potential. You have to limit yourself to that and not think that cinema is able to convey everything about our condition. Its power is its limit, only being able to express our efforts… Where cinema ends, the audience begins: Cinema + audience = One.

The humility of a filmmaker comes from understanding his art well, its imperfection, allowing no vanity and requiring, to give it power, all types of renunciation.

The search for truth is actually an empty word of the mind, and cinema – a modest art – knows, without speech, how to make its orifice visible, felt.

The only truth is the duration of a shot, in other words the rhythm of the film itself: The exposure and the movement of bodies, faces, in time. The rest is naught.

Literature is civil, not cinema. Cinema is *mythical*, it tells the story of how we came to *be*. That is all (nothing more.)

Filming the desert, I film a piece of humanity; in cinema, landscapes are always interior states that remain invisible. Which is where *representation* in cinema comes from, that is to say, art itself: arrived at through other means.

I steal this tree trunk and appropriate it for the mythical needs of cinema.

These pictures were taken during a second scouting trip in California in August 2000. *I seek not, I find*, idem: I always shoot with what already exists, changing nothing, taking what is there, as it is. Am a partisan of the *ready-made*. Scouting is an essential act where I get rid of the representations that came to mind while writing and that do not exist in reality. They are temporary and never last long: they serve to designate objects. This applies to the actors just as much as the decors. EVERYTHING MUST GO. All ideas must disappear: returning to matter, to the shapeless and primitive masses of our sensibility.

No decors, no dialogues, no script: go back to what comes before them. (Cinema is a primal art.)

The different scouting trips (without a camera, at first) serve to overthrow the control of an author and his utopia: imposing reality seen as an object of desire; reality inverts him, overturns him (the author), as the inevitable grasp of matter itself. You must therefore spend a good deal of time, go to these places, wait (for it to come).

Want what happens (Stoic adage).

With time, the cutting (frames, main lines) appears on its own. Cinema, directing, must go through this *unlearning*.

Directing is an asceticism (love of wisdom)

All the preparatory work (writing, scouting, casting actors, casting technicians, storyboarding, trials…) are all exercises aimed at being (on the set, in the editing room) *ready*.

Directing has to implicate itself in this almost *visionary* position, one I find to be so close to ecstasy. You must be ready.

Being a director does not mean making images, but changing them (by filming them).

The actor is an incarnation: he is in himself the substance of the character, his potential. The character has to disappear, he must be eliminated.

Choosing an actor means choosing a character: in other words abandoning the idea of composition. An actor is a ready made, an essential act where all preconceived ideas are abandoned. I direct without ideas because the characters are in front of me: I make adjustments with the actor using what he can do. I watch over him. I watch him being the character and myself wanting what he does. I shape him, fix him = I direct.

I do not direct the actor, but the character himself: modifying him, changing him…

I am now working (*Twenty-nine Palms*) on the dramatic motivations of a story. Trying to establish it more in its energy and its rhythms. Have found a mechanism on which I establish the story and develop it.

Cinema is like drawing: the art of the line, of seizing truth. Each of them are primordial expressions, expressions of life and its movements.

In both sculpture and painting, only the drawing counts, as Giacometti said.

His drawings are never the mark of certainty, they are in turmoil, in the very movement of the form, its activity, with no concepts. *Where do you see lines in nature? There are no lines, just masses that advance or retreat*. He said.

Immobility is the work of the mind, its invention; it is the stumbling block of cinema, its vanity. The body (hushed and animated mass) is the substance of cinema, its energy.

Incompleteness is what resides in nature. Cinema can return to it.

"In truth, the eye of thought does not begin to see acutely until the vision of the eyes begins to lose its sharpness." Plato, *Phaedo*.

Giacometti had a good definition of the problem of human proportions (of their relationships) in representation, finding an expressive response in distance (deformation). The same for Rodin.

7 ▶

8 ▶

9 ▶

Giacometti copied a great deal, as the best way to give an account of what he saw. By copying he knew what he was looking at to a certain extent. There is a resemblance, and then the force of expression because it is a copy.

Most of the scenes I write are copies of traits I have seen and that I then represent.

Reality is the source and the resource of everything.

The work of a filmmaker is to neutralize all the attempts made by each aspect or element of the complexity of the work to dominate or influence it towards a headlong search for harmony, in other words, for fusion.

Search for a beyond, in the monotonous repetition of daily life.

Cinema does not know how to say anything. It does, it acts. Limit to that.

Filming human lives, waiting for it to come…

Give the audience the incompleteness of reality;

no longer believe in the immobility of the world, in any resolution of the mind,

conquer culture, revise our changing existences in the fleeting light of

cinematographic projections. Reside in our knots. Live the illusions of life.

11 ▶

◀12

◀13

◀14

▶ 15

POETICS OF FATALITY

With just two feature films, the strength of individuality of a film-maker has asserted itself against the flow of contemporary French production. Bruno Dumont clearly holds cinema in high regard. He doesn't film reality—though his subject matter has a firm footing in a solid, observed reality—but transcends it to expose, aided by a form that takes on the game of cinematographic representation, what is at the basis of the human being, what motivates him and makes him ultimately tragic. A cinema *of fate (fatum)* which, for now, amounts to *Humanity* (1999), preceded by his first opus, *The Life of Jesus* (1997).

That first film, with its title taken from the book by Ernest Renan that testifies to the nature of the flesh and blood man who gave birth to Catholicism, unfolds in Bailleul, a small town in northern France. It shows the daily life of Freddy, a young man on the dole, living with his mother, epileptic, in love—he says—with Marie. Freddy is going to kill Kader who has a relationship with Marie. A drama of jealousy? A chronicle of everyday racism? What counts is Freddy's remorse and the appeasement he will briefly find at the end of the film by immersing himself in the bosom of nature, which he had never perceived before for its true worth.

With its title, *Humanity* presents itself directly as a total film, asserting a universal pretension. It is not concerned with *Humanity*, but humanity from the fundamental and sacred element which characterises each and every one of us, and that only a few, like the protagonist Pharaon de Winter, know how to reveal to the world and themselves. Once again set in Bailleul, Pharaon is a police officer who leads an enquiry into the rape and murder of a young girl called Nadège. Between Domino, whom he secretly loves, and Joseph, Domino's lover and guilty of Nadège's murder, a terrible impotence weighs on Pharaon's shoulders. It will lead him to take responsibility for the guilt of the people around him who don't know, unlike him, how to draw from a fusional relationship of nature, appeasement and the acceptance of the immense fatality which dominates the human race.

Individuals and common places

The cinema of Bruno Dumont is rich with oppositions which feed the dramaturgy with their conflicts but also, and perhaps above all, provides a place, an interstice for the spectator. The most evident of these dichotomies, the most apparent in the frame, is that which contrasts town and country, city and nature. Places of Man, culture and civilisation, but also the omnipresence of nature that surrounds it, reclaims its ground, and at the heart of which lies both the development and ruin of Man.

Individualistic, *The Life of Jesus* and *Humanity* are both certainly that, in the sense that the solitary man, the one who is not lead astray by the group, can allow himself the mystical act, contemplation, and, *in the end (in fine)*, the awareness of his fatal condition. He is a tragic being but better armed than the group who, caught in the torments of feelings which link individuals, deprives its elements of every capacity for reflection and, thus, for free will. We will come back on that superiority of the individual over the group, but it imposes itself from the start in order to apprehend the particular topography which dominates in both films where the spectator, like the characters, instinctively has the possibility to locate himself.

The streets of Bailleul, in their frontality (*The Life of Jesus*, and *Humanity*) or their laterality (*Humanity*, especially), are quasi-deserts, dotted with occasional pedestrians, inhabitants with their backs to the walls of their houses or seated on their doorsteps, crushed by heat and boredom, similar to big cats protecting their territory and the entrance to their lairs. It's a space they know and control, sometimes going from one neighbour to another, sentries of the bordering territories. Freddy, in *The Life of Jesus*, is king of the street he patrols, and, by his sole presence, rules. On his moped, as the leader, alone at the head, followed by his four mates, he is the Prince of Bailleul. Decidedly slower, it's by bike that Pharaon enters town in a sequence at the beginning of *Humanity*. He too controls his road and knows Bailleul like his pocket. His work as police officer even leads him to restore order to the main square which, not being a street, offers a space for a gathering of angry strikers.

However, if he is evidence of authority alone facing a group, Pharaon remains powerless in his work. His inquiry into the rape and murder of the little girl doesn't progress, despite his willingness. The weight of administration that he represents, a world whose mechanics are routine and allow little room for creativity, hinders him in his individuality. The police station, the recurrent place in the plot of *Humanity*, displays on its walls—not without irony—several notes of intention, from the Declaration of Human Rights to the reassuring portrait of the President of the Republic, along with posters that confirm the popular support the forces of order need. There too, the individual can act: Freddy, "nabbed" for Kader's murder, his rival in love, succeeds without much difficulty in escaping a police station engulfed in its own bureaucratic apparatus. Not shown in any better light than the police milieu, the medical world is, in Dumont's films, a haven of impotence in which men of goodwill, such as the doctor in *Humanity*, find it difficult to express their frustrations. In Pharaon he finds the echo of compassion absent from his own institution. And it's not television, to be found everywhere in that psychiatric hospital, which could procure a short but intense moment of relief for him. The TV screen, that other common place, is disparaged too in *Humanity*, where Pharaon composes a sincere chant on the virtual images of an unnamed war, as well as in *The Life of Jesus*, where Freddy's mother, manifestly a couch potato, prefers the television transmission of the road cycling race than first-hand viewing of that same race a few kilometres away.

The question of the incompetence of the medical world is even more direct in *The Life of Jesus*. It shelters behind its latest tools, scanners as ostensibly impressive as they are incapable to cure or even to explain Freddy's epilepsy. The hospital is, before all else, a place to die for Cloco, Freddy's friend. Suffering from Aids, he agonizes over the total impotence of the medical body.

The museum at Lille, in a sequence in *Humanity*, pays homage to Pharaon de Winter, portrait painter of the Flemish realist school and Pharaon's great-grandfather, with an exhibition that seems an exercise in style for Dumont, framing the painting-shot in CinemaScope. Beyond that appearance resides the vanity of another group, a cultural institution which leaves Pharaon, the uninitiated public, indifferent. There he sees simply the beauty of blue colour and withdraws without paying any more attention to the interest his celebrated ancestor gives rise to.

◄◄ 16

► 17

► 18

These different group places are in a domestication relationship with nature which, automatically, bounds them. The museum, the bastion of culture, is found, of course, at the centre of the big town and thus quite distant from the green hillocks and worked lands which border Bailleul. It is encircled by tar, a few lone trees stand in the streets around the building, and a small area of green grows in the background to the shot of the parking exit from which Pharaon emerges.

The park around the psychiatric hospital is, in *Humanity*, a buffer zone organized into green mown spaces and flowerbeds designed according to the prevaricating convention of the academy-trained gardener. There lies a nature of display, domesticated, where the semi-wild shubbery stands behind their enclosure wall. Segmented by these tarmac paths, the park is perhaps a reflection of the rigid medical institution. It certainly is to its residents, placed under lock and key in its buildings and afflicted with an illness which encloses them in a rudimentary social life along with its artificial relationship with nature.

The garden lying fallow at the police station, a brief insert in reverse shot of Pharaon's empty look—as always—, announces the contrary, the confusion which reigns at the heart of the police force and the erring ways of the enquiry. Each to his own garden. Pharaon's is a small allotment scarcely bigger than his bedroom. He digs it bit by bit with a cautious hand in order to grow in spring, at the end of the film, multi-coloured dahlias somatized by a mental state in naive spiritual—and physical— elevation. We will return to that point. Doesn't Pharaon become one with the rich and fertile land as early as the fifth shot of the film? He submits to nature, humbles himself, asks it pardon. He blends with it and passes through it, avoiding as much as possible to disturb it. Motos and fanfare in *The Life of Jesus*, trains and planes in *Humanity*, all tear into the environment, abusing it. Pharaon drives his company vehicle with the slowness and hesitations of the person who wants to avoid crushing one blade of grass when he leaves the tarmac roads. For, off the roads, nature reclaims its ground, insects appropriate bodies. People leave the road to die (Kader pushed in the ditch in *The Life of Jesus*; Nadège, the little girl raped and murdered whose body is discovered in the middle of a field in *Humanity*…) or, to attempt to die (Freddy, probably eaten by remorse, violently leaves the road on his moped in *The Life of Jesus*). Only Pharaon is tolerated by nature, because he has the humility to understand that it doesn't belong to him. He finds there an already existing representation, with no need to construct it, of his mental state. The ploughed field in the fifth shot in *Humanity* doesn't belong to him. He had to walk to find it and, finding himself in it, he stopped there. It is in that journey, in that crossing of the landscape and the natural elements which compose it, that the spectator, helped by Pharaon's aptitude to contemplation, finds the key into *Humanity*. The slowness of the character and, as a result, of the film, is not a hindrance but, on the contrary, a chance for the spectator to find where he stands. In Pharaon's car, a few diegetic notes of the harpsichord resonate as a benevolent siren which shows him the way. A way he will have to follow at the pace of his character.

Nature is in permanent conflict with Man. He enslaves it, subdues it, tortures it, confines it. Pharaon projects himself into it, a rather personal way to find an echo of his torment nourished by the culpability of others. The impotent groups have, before their eyes, the landscapes they deserve. For Domino, the strong woman with whom Pharaon is in love, and a character prey to her impulses, we should perhaps recall the landscape which appeases her and seems to give her a balance: the sea, in which she immerses the bottom half of her body to urinate while the children play in the water. In that providential and womb-like environment, beauty shines with all the fullness of her massive body and her satiated desires in perfect fusion with nature.

Thus spake Pharaon…

Subject to their impulses, the characters in Bruno Dumont's films sometimes commit the irreparable. A genre plot is generated by them, leading towards a tragedy as the characters become conscious of what determines them and what little freedom their human nature allows them. Sex is the crudest manifestation of that nature. Shot in a very functional way, (organs, faces), it is lived as a pure and simple coupling.

The female characters seem more spontaneously disposed to let their desires speak: in *Humanity* Domino's gaze is irresistibly drawn by the advantages presented by the swimming instructor in his trunks, a friend of Pharaon met by chance; and in *The Life of Jesus* Marie provokes Kader by grasping his hand and drawing it towards her genitalia. Even if they find release in the sexual act, the masculine instincts are far more destructive. For men sex is associated with violent death. Pharaon places himself in such a symbiotic relationship with nature that he becomes incapable of embracing "ordinary" sexual behaviour. Perhaps he doesn't feel the need for it. On the whole, Pharaon doesn't communicate like the people around him. He uses speech economically, giving preference to the other senses, sight and touch mainly, but also smell. His character is

◀ 19

◀ 20

completely sensual, and that sensuality is a door which remains open for the audience throughout *Humanity*.

If the importance of the stagnant social and economic context never appears as a factor to determine the actions (like the absence of a father for Freddy and Pharaon, or the loss of Pharaon's wife and children), the characters set up by Bruno Dumont, according to the obligation of fate, are decked out with defects which form as many handicaps within their groups as potential advantages in solitude. In *The Life of Jesus*, Freddy's epilepsy consumes him, makes him ashamed (*"Do you think I find it amusing to piss on myself?"*) and compels him to have frequent medical examinations. However, each crisis experienced like a little death, the illness gives him the means to realize his crime, to regret it and then to find once more a certain serenity, by accident, in the heart of the natural landscape.

Contrary to Freddy, Pharaon's defect doesn't manifest itself through crisis, but in a more diffused way. Without making him an idiot in the clinical sense, for he remains perfectly rational (he thinks, for example, that Nadège's murder could have been seen from the train), *Humanity* follows Pharaon through his slowness which, alone, seems to give him the means for contemplation, the real key to the film. That defect is clearly stated in the script, and on several occasions. "He's an idiot", remarks an amused fisherman when Pharaon asks him if the catch is good before he has even thrown out his nets. Or, again, an angry striker verbally abuses him when he prevents him from entering the mayor's office. "You're too stupid to be a cop," he tells him. For, if that intellectual slowness brings Pharaon closer to nature and allows him to seize what's natural in a human being, it also defines his professional impotence, giving him no more trumps than his colleagues and his superior have, caught in the machine of the group action and thus, for Dumont, ineffectual. As the idling engine of the plot, Pharaon stigmatises also all that impotence, particularly on the occasion of his point of view shot of a street brawl. In an impossible position to take action, for he is at the top of a building, he has to content himself with the frustrating role of spectator. No doubt he becomes fully aware then of his impotence. Wherever he directs his gaze, he remains a passive observer, except when, from his garden, he contemplates a distant hillock, the only elevated point in the landscape. On arrival at the end of his interior journey towards compassion and humanity, he enters a state of levitation. The humanity, the sacred part in the human being, transcends his body and lifts it a few centimetres.

The sacred here has no relationship with religion. The two are even paradoxical, and Bruno Dumont doesn't leave any doubt as to the distinction he operates: a quick glance by Domino towards the chancel of a church as she crosses before it, seems tainted with irony; one of Freddy's friends comments on the reproduction of a Giotto fresco, *The Resurrection of Lazarus*, hanging on the wall of Cloclo's bedroom agonizing in *The Life of Jesus*, *"It's the man who's resuscitated..."*

The sacred is at the heart of man, not in the heart or chancel of the churches, nor in the sky that Kader looks at, placing his faith in Marie, and where Freddy surrenders, seeking to appease his remorse. A false track, the sacred is among us, here and now. Perhaps on that hill on the horizon, from which Pharaon seems to wait for the return of Zarathustra announcing the death of God. Freddy and Marie on the chairlift crossing the plain, when their relationship is blooming as much as it possibly can, are equally on a superior level, above the others and without physical contact with a nature which, this time (that will happen when they make love in the middle of a meadow), Freddy doesn't abuse.

With their crudeness and naiviety (their innocence?) Bruno Dumont's protagonists are vehicles that go sufficiently slow to make room for their senses. And for the spectator, who doesn't need to intellectualize what he sees here. It is enough to admit the sensuality of the spectacle offered.

The actor and his master

The internal conflicts generated by the impulses of the characters lead *The Life of Jesus* and *Humanity* towards genre film, Série Noire (crime) and Polar (Police) respectively. Directly but, for *Humanity* at least, in slow motion.

In the apparent classicism of a dramaturgy that's respectful of genres, a classical approach of the cinematographic form is associated (by opposition to a modernity of that form, schematically represented in France by the New Wave, but which takes root in Italian neo-Realism): a balance between the number of sequences and shots, fades to black giving structure to the different parts or acts, ellipses... The non-realistic use of sound is an element of that form which, through the mixing, gives preference to the actor's breathe over the surrounding sounds or, on the other hand, accentuates the sounds of nature in contrast to those of men. At the end of the first sequence of *Humanity*, when Pharaon leaves the frame while driving his vehicle, the shot of the

21 ▶

22 ▶

deserted fields and road extends for long enough for the sonorous landscape—the wind, the sound of leaves—to re-possess the frame, like the natural rust that has taken hold of the base of the plough standing in the grass.

The absence of all ontology of shot sequence is also inscribed in that choice of a classic cinema filled with cuts, using a variety of shots and, as we will see, functioning entirely on the exploitation of reverse shot. It is through the natural slowness of Pharaon and through his capacity for a kind of pagan mysticism that, with *Humanity*, Bruno Dumont goes beyond that classicism to reach, curiously, a form of burlesque and what the film-maker himself designates as "poetry". The attributes of the actors have an essential role here. Rough with Freddy, empty with Pharaon, the gaze only has meaning with reference to the reverse shot. The Kuleshov idea, the fundamental discovery of cinematographic technique, established that the quality of the gaze in the shot varies according to what is being looked at in the reverse shot. The extreme and methodic use that Dumont makes of it renders illusory the emotions the spectator reads on the face of a character at the same time as it allows him to insert himself in the interstice, between the scar opened by the shot (Pharaon's gaze) and closed by the reverse shot (Domino and Joseph making love on the living room carpet, the collar of the police captain's shirt covered in sweat, a garden, etc). The CinemaScope and the duration of some shots like the gaze that Pharaon, Domino and Joseph cast on England on the other side of the Channel, make even more permeable to the spectator that suture (the concept of suture, establishing that each filmic shot echoes an absent shot, that the film-maker has the right to present or not, has been established by J. Oudart in *Les Cahiers du cinéma*, n°. 211, april 1969).

The reverse shot is a crucial expectation which demands response. To deprive the spectator of that is not the choice of Bruno Dumont. Each gaze out of shot by Pharaon has its reverse shot, sometimes crude, but it needs to be shown because it exists, a question of morals. The sexual act viewed by Pharaon is thus shown by Dumont, even if it entails shots close to porno films on screen (even more so in *The Life of Jesus*, where the genitals are shown in their functions without anyone watching them).

Other shots must be shown for the plot's needs, even if it doesn't mean positioning the spectator at the character's point of view. That's the case of the shot of the bloody sex of the dead body of the child Nadège, at the beginning of *Humanity*, which will find its suture much later, at the end of the film, when an offered sex is presented, alive and vibrating with all Domino's desire and frustration, shot in the exact same framing as the one of Nadège and always from an extra diegetic point of view. None of the characters make the link between those two shots. It is Dumont in fact who sutures the open slit for the spectator: the object absent from the shot of Nadège's sex is the opposite of that shot, that of the woman prey to her impulses.

If *Humanity* rests mainly on the gaze out-of-shot of Pharaon, Emmanuel Schotté is really the ideal actor. He is not an actor. He doesn't act, but bows to the precise directions of the film-maker. He is, however, contrary to the Bressonian "model", for Dumont models his film on his actor and not the reverse. The Kuleshov idea functions here fully because the film-maker uses the body and the gaze of the actor. Pharaon's behaviour interests him more than his psychology, as he uses his voice more for its timbre and intonations than for what it is liable to express. Pharaon doesn't have anything to say, so he doesn't say anything. Godlike, Dumont shoots him looking left, right, down, rarely up, because there is nothing to see with the exception of, avoiding a play on words, a Mirage. *Humanity* is built on the tight and strange relationship which binds actor and film-maker. A relationship which doesn't exclude the *feedback*, as the jury at the Cannes Festival understood when, in 1999, it gave awards to both the film-maker through the film, and the two main actors, Emmanuel Schotté (Pharaon) and Séverine Caneele (Domino).

Feedback? The perfect actor, for the film adapts to him, reveals a paradox which combines control and the unpredictable. A common phenomenon, but managed by Dumont in his own way. So, in a scene in *Humanity*, Pharaon starts his car, and drives slowly, as is his habit. The close-up shot, framing the character in profile at the wheel, goes on for a long time. Nothing happens, but the shot continues. Then the vehicle runs across an obstacle causing a slight shake The shot stops immediately after that minor event. The film-maker could have cut before that jolt without any need to do that shot again. The shot, already long, would only have lasted a second less. Is it necessary to give a meaning to that jolt? To interpret Pharaon's conduct? A good number of non-justified details remain throughout the film, some unpredictable elements which exist and are therefore kept.

Everything is *mis-en-scene*, accepted in the scene, including the incidents of reality, less through a concern for realism than to find the substance which will feed that famous "poetry", that germinates in *The Life of Jesus*, and is hatched in *Humanity*.

24 ▼

ENQUIRIES ON REALITY

PHILIPPE TANCELIN: *I have watched with great interest* The Life of Jesus *and* Humanity, *both of which you directed, and there seems to me that a very distinct unity is established between the two films. From both an aesthetic and a dramatic point of view, I think the two films clearly complement each other. The theme of death is very present in each. Death comes from crime, and in each case the impulse for this crime springs from a romantic relationship focused on a woman and, on the periphery, sexual acts with very strong sensual tones that can reach extremes, almost to the point bestiality.* Humanity *was filmed after* The Life of Jesus. *With the distance you now have, what do you think is the more profound justification for the order in which things occurred?*

BRUNO DUMONT: I think, and this is the author's point of view, that the second film (*Humanity*) is more mature than the first. In other words, it allows something to be fulfilled that was not there, in my opinion, in *The Life of Jesus*. Something that was not there because maybe I did not try to insist strongly enough on its poetic form, especially for the characters, that is to say, the acting. So I kept a natural form, in appearance, that was a way of starting, maybe of finally making a film. But I knew that I wanted to head off into poetry, into a deformation of reality that I wanted to hear in my ears. That is why the main actor with his very peculiar voice is an essential part of the film's construction. It was something I had already heard at the end of *The Life of Jesus*: the idea for *Humanity* came from the final scene of *The Life of Jesus* when the inspector interrogates Freddy. I had to dub in the inspector's voice because his voice was so poor that it lead the film somewhere else. That was where I wanted to go. I had to take out his voice because I had to finish the film with its own coherence and its own sounds. But I had a character, this completely unreal or surreal inspector, whichever you prefer, and who served as the basis for writing *Humanity*. I have a need to distort reality, conspicuously in this actor's performance. When *The Life of Jesus* first came out, when people starting saying I was a social filmmaker, I said, "Not at all, that doesn't interest me," "that perception of reality is false, it isn't reality"… Well anyway, that was one response to this first film, the political, the social, that I had not intended. My desire was not a collective or a social desire, that doesn't interest me. I have a simpler, more individual, more poetic desire

PT: *They cannot necessarily be separated, and this deformation of reality that you are talking about can accompany a deliberate political, social approach.*

BD: No. At least, there is an appearance of poetry that can lead to politics, if you like, but not initially.

PT: *Your project is not initially political or social, at least in the way these terms are used in those fields. But the poetics you mention could also fulfill that mission.*

BD: I think the way the first film, *The Life of Jesus*, was perceived made me change the way I wrote the second one.

PT: The public's perception or the press?

BD: My own perception as well. But the comparisons made and the things that were said were often wrong.

PT: Like what, for example?

BD: That the film talks about society, about real experiences, about the realities of existence, about unemployment... The film is "false". There are a lot of mistakes, things that are not right and are often inconsistent on a sociological level, like the characters, for example. They don't drink or smoke. They are in a sort of bubble, something that a few viewers noticed like the residents of Bailleul who told me, *"That's not Bailleul! Why did you empty the streets, take everything away? Why didn't you recreate reality?"* But I do not want to film Bailleul; reality is not my project. What interests me is human truth. And, for me, this truth does not pass through the recreation of reality, or in any case, not through the exact restitution of objective reality, but through its alteration. When the actress Marjorie Cottreel, who plays the role of Marie in *The Life of Jesus*, told me for the scene in the park where she undresses: *"That never happens, a girl never does that!"*, it is not important because I am well aware that no one ever does that. But that is precisely what cinema is, going farther. When I do that I am satisfied, I know I am doing cinema. I also know that I have to stay very close to reality because there is a necessary proximity between reality and truth. That's why I think *Humanity* goes a little farther towards unreality with a character who is always on the edge. Is he really a policeman or not? Some people think so, others not, etc., so much the better. I am very interested in this kind of ambivalent game.

PT: Coming back to your remark "this is not social cinema", I would like to be provocative and say that it questions social and political experience from a new point of view. That seems obvious, even though a total interpretation is possible.

BD: A contrario, there is a need for appearances. However, I take "real" people and trained actors do not satisfy me because I need reality, real decors, real people, real sounds to create fiction. I never think of making fiction with artificial means. I spend all my time trying to keep the set designers from repainting things because I've chosen the decor and nothing should be changed; we are shooting, not repainting. When costume directors ask me how to dress characters, I say "let's go to their closet and take their clothes." All these questions from the technical crew around me raise this problem. The choice, and not the object, is decisive. I also think there is something inaccessible. I am in the process of making a film and finding means of expression and the audience is on the other side. I do not expect us to agree and am much happier with the pleasure the audience may have in finding some meaning, even if it is light years away, no matter, this isn't totalitarian cinema. There is no message, no communication. It should be poetic, sensual, in order to allow different views to form freely. All the most precise and rational discourses on these films are the ones that upset me the most because I am a filmmaker, not of the collective, but of the individual., I don't know what the collective is. For me, a collective is filled with individuals. Pharaon is the subject of *Humanity*; in *The Life of Jesus*, Freddy is the subject. That is the point of departure, and all the directing focuses on them. For my next film, *The end*, the main subject is an individual. So precisely the question of *Humanity*, of directing comes into play. How can one talk about a man today with all the baggage that fills an audience's mind, in our mind and how can one find a place next to that. At the same time, I have nothing to say except what I am doing, nothing else. I do not like to start speaking at the end of a projection. I do not make films about discussions, beliefs or any ideology. I am someone trying to do cinema, to understand cinema, but not like a filmmaker who asks the question and then thinks… What is cinema? I don't care about that. I am trying to make films, so that each time all the elements that I set to work find a harmony and form a body that resonates. That is what I am looking for. I would rather have spectators return to the physical world, because since cinema is physical. It is hard to talk about physical things, but why not, even if only to speak poorly. Discourse bothers me, ideology bothers me. That is why I was talking about poetry at the beginning of the interview.

PT: This poetics is very clear. And it evokes music even more since there are fewer dialogues than rhythms, tempos…

BD: It is musical. You can find the elements that make up music: melody, rhythm, harmony. There's that. That is what I am looking for; however, there is no music. With sound, with a shot, it becomes music. You are in something that belongs to music. Cinema is an art of synthesis that comes after the others and, also, comes before all the others because I think that it the art that is closest to life. You see real people, you hear real sounds. Not in painting. Not in literature. Cinema is even rawer and might transmit a certain knowledge, an experience to the spectator that is perhaps the strongest we can do. Many films today are only illustrations of statements, ideas or texts while others like myself are trying to develop a rawer cinema. That's right, raw.

PT: But not realist.

BD: No, I am not a reality filmmaker, but rather someone who is looking for "truth". And I do not expect anything from reality. Reality doesn't teach me anything. The evening news on television tricks us into thinking we are well informed, but we are better informed by going to a movie theater. I think that is where information can be found. Television news programs foster an unnatural relationship.

PT: I think that approach can be seen clearly in The Life of Jesus, *an approach I would call an "aesthetics of the sign", where everything is a sign of something else, but where the sign only refers to itself.*

25 ▶

BD: Yes, but because I think cinema is a means of expression, that everything is a sign for something else. As a spectator, the films that touch me are the ones made by auteurs where what I see says something else. As soon as the image or the scene only speaks for itself, I find it really boring. A means of expression is when what we see means something else. And it belongs to the audience. Which means that the audience has meaning and that they are, in fact, what makes cinema possible.

PT: We can talk about more obvious signs like the wild car in The Life of Jesus, *for example, which also returns in* Humanity *in the shape of a truck. They can be interpreted in different ways—signs of death, of fate—the essential remains: our perception of them is more intuitive than conscious.*

BD: Yes, and there are tragic signs, ironic ones, playful ones, etc.; and, they coexist.

PT: Everything seems to point to a certain inevitability, that things happen with no necessary causal relationship. That things are thus and that nothing can counteract this situation, at least when observed from a rational point of view.

BD: It is profoundly dogmatic. In other words, a filmmaker is someone who relies on something that is not soft, something like a violent determinism.

PT: We do not know what will happen, but something is prepared that might not conclude but is developing.

BD: When I am filming, I feel a strong, gigantic fatality. By fatality, I mean that I know I am filming even things that bother me but I know that it is written, that I have to film them. So I don't ask any questions, even if those things bother me and I film them without hesitating because it is written. There is no way to escape it. I also tell the actors, "*That's the way it is.*" Even the acting is sometimes very restricted; the actors are placed in danger. For example in the travelling shot where Freddy is riding a scooter at the beginning of *The Life of Jesus*, I told the driver that we weren't going fast enough. He said it would be dangerous. I replied, "It may be dangerous, but we are going too slow, and therefore the shot is not true. We have to go faster." Some of the limitations that disturb me often come from technicians who tell me that something is not possible, that it is too dangerous, that it will fall down… But it has to be true; it has to be accurate. So let's take the risk.

PT: In the film The Life of Jesus, *as in* Humanity, *all the elements are gathered together so that something can happen. We do not know or guess how they will potentially be accomplished but we can tell that there is a meaning in their accomplishment. And that this meaning establishes the inevitability.*

BD: Yes, it has meaning, for example, *The Life of Jesus*. It means extending this title into a person's life and into the modernity in which we live.

PT: This wandering leads Christ out of his character and spreads into the people who appear and whom he questions about their own characters...

BD: He is not a character because he is not incarnate. Christ does not exist himself; he is only the expression of a meaning.

PT: But here we are in the wandering of a meaning that is no longer looking for what must be accomplished but that is accomplished purely gratuitously, ignoring its object.

BD: This same question is treated in *Humanity*, the question of evil. The films that I make confront evil. They do not respond to it. Do not respond to it at all. In other words, they do not engage in reasoned discourse. That is why you have these titles: *The Life of Jesus, Humanity*. They are both conceptual or given a meaning whereas the means of expression are not, or no longer have meaning. Maybe that is what cinema is: a body, flesh, wind, even with a vain title. At the same time, the film itself demolishes the vanity of the title. I think, at least I hope so!

PT: All of this discussion refers us to another reading, or at least another approach to History that is quite different from the one we can get from a linear conception of time where History is written by a certain arrangement of events. For you, it is the event...

BD: Do you mean history with a capital H?

PT: Yes.

BD: But that is where History means the least and where fiction, telling a story is much more powerful, much stronger. All the documents you can discover concerning the concentration camps will never be as powerful as a fictional work. The problem is human truth, not reality. This truth is the goal of fiction. Fiction speaks about it and reveals it. That's why you can get bored and not cry when watching images of war and finally lose all interest, whereas something fictional can make you cry. It is not a question of the image, but of the spectator. His or her emotion counts the most. The problem nowadays is that we are inured to the monotony of television images that have no more impact, while fiction is able to tear us away from that.

PT: Coming back to The Life of Jesus, *there is no determinism, but there is something that develops inevitably through crime, love, friendship... Something that we cannot escape, though without realizing it.*

BD: Yes, but that is the script itself. There is no freedom because everything is written.

PT: Do you think there is no escape?

BD: In cinema?

PT: No, in reality?

BD: No. And that is why cinema is not reality. They're not the same at all. All this talk about interactive cinema, I think it's quite foolish. Who should or shouldn't die? No one cares. The audience does not need interactivity, it needs meaning and needs to confront this meaning, to turn off the television set, to live with it or not. That is what makes our job great. I believe that there is an enigma in each work and that the presence of the audience holds the promise of meaning. But they have to sketch it out as well. That is why you need to leave a place for the audience.

PT: Let me come back to the common points between The Life of Jesus *and* Humanity. *There is crime, death, love…*

BD: In *The Life of Jesus* and *Humanity*, there is evil; and in *Twenty nine Palms* and *The end*, my next films, it's the same. There is evil and there is love. But all films talk about those things. The question of evil, of love, of instinct, of freedom and of fate. The question is: what freedom do we have?

PT: And it's a card game where the game, and not the cards, determines the result.

BD: I think we are pushed into love and pushed into crime. We are all in the same situation. We are capable of love and capable of evil. All of my characters are caught in that situation…

PT: Like Jesus moving between the two…

BD: Yes and, when it is not completely without hope, the end of any film, I think, is never completely dark.

PT: No, since one of the characters meditates on the clouds…

BD:… And on the landscape because he is not looking at the clouds at the end of the film, but the landscape, since there is no transcendence. It is not found up there but down here. The solution is to be found in the landscape… It is an awakening and the word awakening seems right. You have to wake up and find the strength. We need to find strength in art works in general, strength that will help us as individuals. The individual is important, not the work.

PT: Is this awakening a passage into others?

BD: It is the passage into oneself. It means releasing oneself to oneself. I have had revelations in front of works of art, not immediately, it took time and they helped me understand and live. Works of art are not important in themselves and you have to be rather humble about what a film is.

PT: Isn't that true for any work of art to the extent they are only a reception area and have no vocation to lead?

BD: Yes. Vanity must be avoided, and that isn't easy. The hardest part is getting away from vanity, moving towards simplicity. That is where work comes in. Vanity is what comes first. Someone simple is someone who has done a great deal of work. The endpoint of a work is not complexity but simplicity, of a shot, of a figure… The most beautiful films I have seen are also the simplest. They are powerful, but there is nothing there.

PT: This simplicity that you find so touching, which directors do you think master it?

BD: There were films by artists when I was a student where I saw a lot of films. Films by Kubrick, Bergman, Resnais, Fellini, Ferreri... Blier. Yes, artists. I saw films that were made by auteurs, people who used cinema as a means of expression. And I left the theater without understanding everything, like when I saw Providence by Resnais, but I liked it. Or there were exotic films that made me want to make films. I haven't had that feeling in a long time.

PT: Is that what made you want to make films?

BD: Expressing myself, writing is something I wanted to do very early on. I wrote screenplays. Luckily I made my first film at 37, otherwise it would have been horrible! It was too vain. That's how I feel today when I look at some of my short films and often see pretentious intentions. You have to purify because this is an art that does not allow the slightest pretentiousness.

PT: With your concern for simplicity and purified images, shots, acting, what is your position on the Dogma theories developed by some of the filmmakers of your generation? They seem, according to their principles, to be working on themes that are close to yours. Such as simple characters, often personified by a retarded person, images that avoid being artificial with cameras set in place that capture the scene as it develops during the time of the take, a refusal of artificial sounds by only using those produced by the action without any extra ambiance.

BD: But these principles, they can already be found in Rossellini. If they want to turn them into a dogmatic and almost industrial discourse today, well...

PT: You don't think it forms an aesthetic position?

BD: It is not a new one... It is at least an asceticism. But, if I dare say so, it's a lost cause. Because it is violent, totalitarian. It is violent from a political point of view to declare rules. But the film industry, Hollywood are also rules. Filming poor people does not make it worthwhile. The expresssion gives something value more than saying you are going to film without lighting. Filming poor people will not provide you with a truth you wouldn't have in filming the upper middle class. That's not true. The unveiling determines its price.

PT: These questions, that we can approach through your films The Life of Jesus *or* Humanity, *how do they appear in the film you are currently working on,* The end?

BD: It is above all a detective film... but a decadent one. There are a number of fantastic elements, science fiction aspects, all the paraphernalia of American films with earthquakes, special effects, heroes, etc. *The end* makes something unfamiliar out of the familiar. The familiar, the givens are the hero, the character, the plot, the secondary characters, the paranormal events that are part of the Hollywood mythology, even the

◀ 26

screenplay. The character leaves the place where he is from to move through another environment from which he falls. He is alienated. He and the others are all alienated, extreme people. When you see representations of American cops, they have become fundamentally insane. What makes the character tragic, as opposed to American cops who rarely have a clear idea of who they are, is that he is conscious of his situation. This makes it a tragedy, because he is alienated and he is aware of this alienation that makes him human, I think, and makes him a touching character. For me, that makes him a cinematic character.

PT: When will you start filming?

BD: I have done a good deal so far since I have already scouted locations, but it will depend on the casting. If everything goes well, the project will take place in the next two or three years. In *The end*, there is more of a search for new means of expression, their renewal. I am really searching for them. As soon as I think of a scene, it's *"what does it mean?"* Especially since I can't see it, since it isn't visible. As a moviegoer, if I see what it is expressing, it is worthless, there is a problem.

PT: So there is always a question that remains in suspense for the audience, the question of its place in the image?

BD: I am searching. When I wrote *The end*, it was, how can I express this, maybe still the same thing, but in a different way. The obsessions might still be the same, but above all not the means of expression. And then I am preoccupied with the presence of the audience. I make films with an audience. So I know that someone is there and that there are a lot of things I don't need to do. I really like this conversation with spectators; and progress for a filmmaker might be saying less and less. The greatest films are the simplest ones because the audience really exists in them and the film completes their desire. The worst films are closed, they already contain everything and leave nothing to do. A closed film. There are so many films like that.

PT: In this sense, as you were saying, Humanity *seems to be more accomplished than* The Life of Jesus. *For what seems to differentiate fundamentally* The Life of Jesus *from* Humanity *is that in the latter you proposed plans of thought. There are many fixed shots, very few travelling shots… It is as if you were asking the viewers to build their own images to move away from the very interpretation of what you provide. An exemplary scene, for me, is the one where a chaffinch is reduced to a shadow through which we hear the recording. All of a sudden, the image no longer refers to a specific reality.*

BD: A film is a means. It is a passage, an intermediary. But what is most difficult in constructing a film is writing: a film is thinking, it is thought, it is a mental operation, and that has to be broken down by cinema. Cinema, for me, is not the mind. I know I have to eliminate my thoughts. So keeping my camera still is a way of eliminating myself. I film detached. I know I have to disappear and have everything form a block, turning the film

◄ 27

◄ 28

29 ▶
30 ▶▶
31 ▶
32 ▶▶
33 ▶
34 ▶▶

◄ 35

◄ 36

into an object itself after everything else has disappeared. I push everything, and everyone, to humility so that what appears is the film itself and so that no virtuosity comes through in the camera movements, the actors. I often cut shots that are too pretty, scenes where the acting is too good... All that has to be broken down, it is discordant. I think I learned that from looking at paintings, in other words, that the idea must be eliminated. Real painting occurs when the painter eliminates the idea, since when you paint, you are driven by an idea and all the work consists in dissolving it.

PT: In this light, there is a strong reference to painting in Humanity. *The corpse of the adolescent girl in the grass evokes* Etant Donné *by Duchamp...*

BD: So I am told, but I only saw it for the first time last week, so it wasn't a conscious reference. *L'Origine du Monde*, yes, but Duchamp, no. But I don't always like finding references like that. I even think it is a mistake, like the shot called *L'Origine du Monde*. Cinema is not painting. It comes before painting in my view.

PT: But there, it was not on purpose...

BD: I know the things I have done are imperfect and am well aware of it. I have to get away from literature, from the too well written, the too well said, the author's touch... All that must be broken down. Even if cinema is a synthesis of many arts, they still must be broken down each time. Shots that are too perfect, anything too photographic, literary, theatrical, architectural or pictorial in a shot's composition, all that has to be eliminated. Cinema has to eliminate it. Well, anyway, I have made mistakes and when I see them, it bothers me. The shot of Domino's genitals as she cries at the end of the film is too close to something I am familiar with...

PT: What is it that bothers you so much?

BD: The reference to *L'Origine du Monde*. It bothers me, and having people tell me about it bothers me. Your reference to Duchamp doesn't please me either. But I can only refer to the audience's culture. People tell me, "*It reminds me of the place I'm from, of my brother...*" At the same time, it can't be avoided. The audience is not neutral and it is there. That is why I'm saying that the viewer has to be incorporated even more and that my films should not carry a connotation, such as "this means that, etc.," like in caricatures or comedy. I can see that viewers change and their sensibilities evolve, which means that I have to evolve since I am in placing myself in relationship with them. My films have to change. The questions being asked today are precisely about the evolution of the audience, of cinema... Those are my current preoccupations.

PT: Is there also a didactic project combined with this idea of the evolution of the audience?

BD: Didactic project?

PT: In terms of the audience...

BD: No, there is a project to establish contact. I have to be in contact. There are people who, a priori, do not come to see the film, it does not interest them. Something disturbs them, I guess… something keeps them from coming. Moviegoers today go to a movie theater because we have a mass, industrial cinema, a consumer cinema. An artist today is someone who has to incorporate a certain amount of the data that exists today in order, if I may say so, to establish contact. So the film I am preparing is a film where I say, "If you want x, here it is." I take it to give them this contact. I will be using the contact as a means of expression. It won't change anything. If I have to use a well-known actor, I can do that. I will see if it works better and if it doesn't, I will do something else. I have been thinking about this a lot. But for me this contact is a means of expression, even if there is a cynical relationship with the actor.

PT: Aren't you giving in to pandering to the audience?

BD: No, I think that the audience has to give a little and so does the author. You cannot make a film by turning your back on the public. In certain cases, you can do that too, there are filmmakers who choose to do that, but I think experimentation is necessary. I have only made two films, and I am trying to make a third by changing things. I don't want to be put in a niche and do my thing in a corner. I think there are risks that should be taken, aesthetic, artistic and economic risks as well. When I hear twenty year-olds telling me, "*It's so slow, so long,*" I don't think they are right, but there is something… when I see what they see and what they like.

PT: Are you comforted to hear them say that, given what they watch and when what you offer them surprises them, even if it is a violent surprise.

BD: I want to be in touch with them. Not to go with the flow, but just to establish a relationship with their codes, their sensibility, with the universe in which they live. Yes, to capture their attention. Once they are in the theater, then it's my business. They can leave, that does not bother me. But if they decide not to come, then I think there is a problem.

PT: How do you know that they decide not to come?

BD: Because I look at the ticket sales…

PT: Because what you offer is a different experience of time, of duration, of causal relationships between events and twenty year-olds, not all of them by the way, "disconnect" more rapidly. And because, if they are given continuous motion shots like in Oliveira, whom I personally admire, they get bored?

BD: Film is a means of expression and one that does not work with them. They do not accept it.

PT: Not all of them though?

BD: No, but they are desensibilized, subject to a deformation of sensibility that comes from the ways they consume cinema—or food, it's all the same. Their relationship to cinema is a convulsive one, rapid, musical. A filmmaker must be able to incorporate their language as well… And, at the same time, they have a language that is not necessarily the same as mine. So "This is your language," therefore, "I am going to talk like you." But to capture their attention, lead them elsewhere. I think *Humanity* can be convincing, but people still have to go see it, watch it. A spectator who tells me, "*I came because someone forced me to, etc. I didn't want to come but it was really good,*" there is nothing better. Someone who is already convinced before it starts interests me less. Maybe it's the mindset of the conqueror. But conquering spectators interests me because it forces me to change my approach. In the 1970s/80s, there were filmmakers who were able to be both universal and profound. Today, I think that age is over in the sense that the public is no longer made up of film aficionados; it consists of consumers. And if you still want to make films, I tend to tell myself that they have a language and this is it. *The end* is a film that in its form and appearance—but at the same time, it is an illusion—in its distribution and in its production attempts to correspond to what the public expects, apparently.

PT: How do you account then for your desire for contrivance?

BD: But it is contrivance. It occurs when you extend your hand to someone. Afterwards, the film takes over; there are risks to be taken. In any case, it means not chasing people away. Not going against what people desire today or what they want to see.

PT: Don't you think that this position could be taken as a concession with its accompanying resignation, denial or a certain opportunism?

BD: No, on the contrary. My intention is to change things but with new parameters in this case. I will always try to alter but in a more cynical way, one that plays with the audience's toys, since they need their toys. They want to see a certain type of story; my intention is therefore to act but to alter this conception. I am not an industrial filmmaker, I don't know how to do that. But I am able to take their favorite actor and do something else. That is a contrivance I like. There is no difference between an American movie star and Emmanuel Shotte. They are beings who embody something. This time I want to work with a star, in other words with someone who embodies something. There is an absolutely incredible relationship with the desire to identify that we cannot control. I want to capture the audience by taking their star and bringing them to me with that appearance. This does not mean taking them and pouring myself into them, of course not, but it means not making films against them. I am more interested in fact by people who don't like my films than by those who do. And I can tell that they dislike them because they are not adjusted in the same way.

PT: Do you think it is a question of adjustment and not a fundamental political or economic problem that contemporary artistic production is increasingly giving in to the market and "communicability"?

BD: I think it is vain to think you can reach everyone. That is not what I am looking for. However, I believe in the universal, I think we can reach something large. I am lucky enough to make films that are understood in America, Asia, Europe. There is a sincere relationship, a strong one. And I want to see if it is a possibility today or if I have to give up. If I have to give up because I am wrong, well, I will just stop reaching out.

PT: In The Life of Jesus *and* Humanity, *you did not want to reach out, you were looking for more of a spiritual contact.*

BD: Yes, and the two are not contradictory. This is not a problem of depth, which is inherent in everything I do. I do not want to be superficial. I want to be sincere. But, it's a language problem. It's as if I were talking to someone who doesn't speak the same language. I am trying to speak the other language a little. That is what I have been trying to tell you. That is all I have been intending to do. It is not a concession.

PT: Did the "actors" in Humanity *and* The Life of Jesus *sense this contrivance?*

BD: Completely, they are means of expression. So they might have felt a sort of distance that relieved them of their own view of themselves and, at the same time, they are caught up in a fate that is beyond their control. They are characters. I am not looking to start with a fusion with the actors, and I tell them. I steal things from them, I do not try to make them understand, to have them agree with what I am doing; all that is not important.

PT: Certainly, I don't think one should attempt fusion with actors and actors steal from the director just as much as he steals from them and that should be said. Concretely, how did you deal with them when you were shooting the films?

BD: We merely trusted each other.

PT: It still seems like you interact with them on a very playful level...

BD: Yes, play. Above all, I redirect, I distort. I do not need reality, in other words a meaningful shot. I know that I will edit, I know that I can cut even if things are not going well in the sequence I am shooting. Completion takes place during the editing. I even have a feeling of mediocrity during the shooting. I tell Emmanuel, "You are thinking about your wife," and during the editing I stick Séverine in front of him. It's cheating, but I am looking for truth. When I shot the scene where Marie is making love with Freddy, I twisted her foot. I knew that her suffering would be an image of pleasure. I do not have to ask her to pretend. I do not need that particular truth. They are in the processes of making a movie and movies are a trick. It's the famous Koulekov effect: *"think about whomever you want... think about an apple...."* No one cares about thinking about the

meaning. There is no intellectual relationship to the meaning of a scene. If I want to make an actor cry, I look into his or her own life and during the editing it evokes something else. But I don't want to make actors cry because of what I write... they couldn't care less. I love doing that. In *Humanity*, I did it even more... distorting shots, meanings... thinking or saying something else, knowing all the while what I wanted to do with it. The relationship I have with the actors is even a distant one but making them say something that will become something else, where the editing becomes a new reality, all that fascinates me. At the same time, there is something fake, like in painting, but I think we can reach the truth through falsehood. There is something artificial, fictitious, altered, deceitful about it but that's what artistic expression is. And that is not where the truth is found... Sometimes when I look at the rushes, I am shocked, nothing is happening. But during the editing, it works. I think that even mediocrity has something in reserve for the editing. Otherwise, if it is good, there is nothing to edit. Filming an actor acting handsome... you take the first shots and then I have nothing to do. I prefer having awkward things and then digging, scraping and editing it all; it's fascinating. I can tell that I have an increasing desire to work with awkwardness, with waste, the little things that break, the falls, the accidents... To a certain extent, when I say "action", I don't know what is going to happen. I wait and watch. I want an accident to occur.

PT: Do you cause accidents?

BD: Yes, I cause them and I do not use my script as a model. I don't ask the actors to go towards the script. On the contrary, the script is the impulse. When I saw Emmanuel walking with his hands like that, towards the rear, that was good. But I never wrote that. He has a unique way of walking. I am interested in whether it is right, right for him. I don't want to throw him off.

PT: Even returning a certain cinematic accuracy to him...

BD: The accuracy of what he himself expresses. He becomes an instrument and I have to find and protect his balance. He has to be good; he has to do it right. He has his own rhythm, his own way of speaking. I think I understood what he was like and so I just made adjustments: less, more, faster, slower, softer, louder. At the same time, there is a certain compositional work that takes place but starting with him; he is the body and flesh of this work. He is always composing; he wants to know what he should say, where he should go, etc. I tell him what to do and he does it, but he is acting.

PT: So you do give your actors a lot of directions?

BD: Yes, very much so. There is no improvisation because they do not know how to improvise. They always ask, *"What should I say, what should I do?"* I cannot reply, "You figure it out," because then they figure it out and do nothing. I say "action" and they don't move. And they don't have the script so I don't tell them their lines. I tell them the intention. They end up learning it, but to a certain extent they never get it. They never

read it. So I talk with them just before the scene and give them motivations for what they are going to say. But they are the ones that speak and can change a certain aspect.

PT: So you do tell them the story…

BD: Obviously. When the mother says, "*Mom is not happy,*" she is the one who says it. I tell her, "You say you are not happy." I don't say, "Here are your lines," but "You explain that you are not happy." I give the impulse…

PT: In fact, they practically write the dialogues themselves using their idea or their intuition of your imagination.

BD: Yes. But when you read the script, you find exactly what is written.

PT: Except in Humanity *where there is more of a discrepancy…*

BD: Yes, I cut out a good deal because there are always things that are no good, that do not work. During editing, I do not insist on keeping everything. Accuracy is necessary. Everything that is not right is eliminated. There are scenes that were very scripted but where the actor wasn't good. The father of the victim says "No" when they visit him, there was a line but he couldn't say it. So he ended up saying just "No," the end of his text. That is fine. I watch the scene, rehearse it, hear what doesn't work, then I take it out, eliminate, eliminate and all that is left is the "No" that is quite beautiful. So, that's what we do. I do not rehearse scene after scene with him. It is a type of freshness.

PT: Pharaon's sexuality, which is very pronounced in the script of Humanity, *was absent from the film. But there is a trace that you can sense without seeing it.*

BD: Because first of all the actor refused the sexual relations. I explained to him that I could cheat with the act, get a stand-in. He didn't accept it. So the character of Pharaon who was supposed to very sexual was relieved of his sexuality through an actor's choice. I could have not chosen him, but I wanted him. I was the one who abandoned, "I prefer having you and accepting you the way you are." And when I watch the scene today, I think it works well. Normally, at the end of the script when he kisses Domino, he was supposed to have sex. That does not happen and it was an accident. When I said the script was fated, it's because there are things I abandon since that is part of the film. I wrote the film *Humanity* for the cop who was in *The Life of Jesus*, but he never wanted to do it because his wife didn't want him to… And, well, I found someone else who was different. Emmanuel was "fuller"… But, he also had the uneasiness I wanted. He was someone else who sounded different, so I listened to the way he sounded and then incorporated him.

PT: This displacement, this other place where you lead actors by your suggestions, has that had an effect today on their life experiences?

BD: Yes. We have such an intimate relationship… In reality, we wouldn't touch each other, but I touch them, grab them, put them over there. The directing itself with the crew creates this proximity. We enter inside the characters, and inside the crew too, and it works wonders because you don't do that in real life. Because of this proximity, they have a very strong experience, humanly speaking, not because of the film but because of the process of making it. I think that fulfills all our desires as people who are together on a set. "This is a different place, we are not doing the things we usually do and it's refreshing," is what they say each time.

PT: Are they reticent to the director's approach or do they, on the contrary, try to find a certain harmony or resonance?

BD: I make myself understood. My approach is very simple, "you walk, you do…." I do not need them to understand me. It is not important whether they understand the meaning. They need to understand where they are going, what they are doing, what is happening… All the rest… So I say things simply and it's good not to get too worked up. I think I even end up leaving the screenplay behind.

PT: Have you ever let a scene go on and then use it in the end?

BD: Of course. Since there is not much dialogue, I wait. I can tell that my camera is waiting and that the position of the camera, even in *Humanity*, is waiting for whatever happens. During this wait, I can see things that come out and yet nothing happens, I see that very quickly in the rushes. I remember filming a very simple shot where I said, "You go over the fence and walk through the field." He jumped over the fence and walked through the field. Three days later, I watched the rushes and there was something else there. Something that the camera had done. It was no longer just a guy jumping the fence and walking. So I know that when I am filming, I have to do as little as possible, shoot nothing. To a certain extent, the more I film nothing, the more elements I have to edit. And all the pretentiousness of dialogues, all that, I don't like. Already "speaking" keeps something from happening. But talking is necessary and the words are purely factual, *"what should we do?"* They don't express anything in the sense that they might be a vehicle for something. However, I have written words and as soon as I hear something "thoughtful" I cut because it is uncomfortable. I cannot, physically, bear hearing something that serves as a meditation. Everything that meditates on an action, where the actor meditates on what he is doing, seems completely wrong to me. So I take it out. And when I tell you that there is still dross lying around, it means that my elimination wasn't well done. For me, it's an error, a defect.

PT: Your approach to the actors, since they are not professional actors, seems to resonate with the approach of certain directors in theater. I am thinking of C. Bene and his concern for the becoming-actor of each one of us. Allowing the time necessary, not for something to occur but for each subject to develop in the time provided. This approach is often more theatrical than cinematic.

BD: Cinema suffers from the "star system" and from the idea that actors are products

◄ 42

◄ 43

that are reused for purely economic reasons. It also suffers from actors' control over directors that has almost neutralized directing. In my opinion, as a director, it's like a massacre to watch all these actors come back, always the same... Physically, I cannot stand the presence of an actor I have already seen. Something there eliminates the desire for new discoveries. There is something in the work, in the composition that still escapes me for the moment. I have been much too disappointed by working with actors, with their composition and the difficulty that must precisely be found. My decision to use non-professionals is a completely radical decision that springs from my deep deception in the relationships I have had with actors... not being able to do it. I do not blame the actors, it's me. No matter. But I hear them and it doesn't work in my ear.

PT: Is it a question of sound?

BD: Yes, there is something inappropriate, illusory, that does not feel right in my ear. And when I see actors act, that is what I think. I do not believe them.

PT: Wouldn't that be the poetic dimension of your films? That there is something incompatible and that is not only a question of individuals or of the actor's training but also, perhaps, of the social scene on which they are asked to perform, to display themselves. The actor does not embody the poet; it is poetry that embodies the actor in a new way so that he can find his human voice before his acting voice. Is that how you feel, this absence, this difficulty in dealing with "professional" actors?

BD: The work I do with non-professional actors is exactly the opposite. I write a character and then I reduce my character to the actor. Whereas a professional actor composes starting with what he is, what he can do, what he knows how to do, to build towards the character, with me, under my eyes, asking if it works like this, etc. I do not know how to do that or I have no ideas about the character, which is a strong possibility. When I work, I think I take steps towards them. I do the work of reducing myself to them, the movement that an actor probably makes towards a character. I give up a lot of things to want what he is, who decides, who says it is good. I want what he is. I can say, "That's good, that's no good," but I can't say that ten times to an actor! He can only offer me what he is doing, or maybe a little more, a little less. Professional actors offer me too many things and I get lost, I won't know what to do... I don't know. With non-professional actors, there is no alternative except choosing between one or the other.

PT: Your decision to work with non-professionals comes from the fact that they do not overact...

BD: Because their internal clockwork is true. And my desire is for truth. Actors, they are searching, and actors who search fatigue me. I don't know. I cannot help them. It's something I don't know how to do. God knows I have spoken with actors, *"Do you want me to do it like this or like that?"* I don't know.

◀ 44

◀ 45

◀ 46

47 ▶

◀ 48

◀ 49

PT: What shocks you is that actors claim that the raw and immediate proposals they make are an incarnation of the truth...

BD: It is always a question of truth, always truth. At the same time, I think that the truth does not exist. It appears through an individual perspective. I am not on a quest for absolutes... I've stopped searching. So, a decor is necessary and, well, this one will do. That is why I never ask decorators to create a decor because I have no idea what I want. So I choose an apartment and say, "This is it. We're filming here." That's how it works. I am not going to say, "Hey, let's paint this blue," ever. With an actor, it's the same. If he is there, he is there, period. He is blond, good! I would never say, "We have to dye his hair." In *Humanity*, Séverine was missing a tooth. I would never say, "We need to add a tooth." Too bad, I want to keep it. He is like that, he walks like this, I incorporate it. I have to pay attention to coherence, to harmony, that is my job. But I can say "no", I can say "cut". I would stop if what I was doing wasn't right. It is not a naive vision of whatever is said. No, I work with them. I can stop them, correct them, cut them off...

PT: What determines these starts and stops? What structure of "coherence"?

BD: By the actor's construction, his musicality. I listen to him, and as soon as he is discordant, I can hear it. I remember that the first scene I did with Emmanuel is the one where he goes to see the bus and walks around it. I watched the way he walked, the way he spoke. I incorporated it; it's the instrument. I know how he can sound. I listen. My directing only uses his possibilities. However, he can be off, and when it is false, then it means I was wrong or that I asked him to do something he did not know how to do. If he doesn't know how to do it, I cut it. Sometimes there are sentences that actors do not know how to say. In those cases, I can't put up a fight forever. But "since you don't know how to say it, how would you say it?" "I would say it like this." If the meaning is there, it's alright. It's an eternal negotiation, but I am intransigent. I don't start him off by saying, "Express yourself!" Since they have nothing to express, the problem is irrelevant.

PT: When you say: "I don't start him off"...?

BD: I don't say, "Go on, improvise!" No! But I watch him grow, develop within the limits I have established. But he does the developing, that is his job as an actor. I watch him work, I listen, and I tell him it's good if I like what he embodies in his own development. But not mine, not at all! The idea of the timbre is not mine, it is his. The decisive part is the choice I make. When I choose someone, I go all the way. He or she becomes the character. Whatever they do, exaggerating a little bit, is still them. Nevertheless, since there can be awkward moments from time to time, I pay close attention. Sometimes I say, "No, what you just did there is no good." From experience, I can get everything, get everything from them, under the conditions I spoke about earlier... They can cry. They will act. They will do it.

PT: Are they acting when they cry?

BD: No, they are really crying. They aren't acting anymore, they do not know that, but you do not have to explain it to them. They only cry if I go get personal events from their lives. When Séverine cried, I was telling her, "Think about your grandmother…" We only worked on her grandmother. The film didn't matter. You have to cast about inside them, they are human beings and so they have everything inside them; joy, suffering, everything is there. They can only produce it from their own experience and not from me, the person who just wrote the screenplay.

PT: So they have a veritable aesthetic experience, with both identification and distance as in life.

BD: Yes, perhaps, but I know that it will be sincere. I go searching for their joy, their suffering and they will give it to me. At least that is the risk I take! And if they don't want to, then I have problem. Like when Emmanuel said no sex, I can't do that. Why? Because his wife did not want him to and he did not want any problems with his wife. She is always there and I know that I have to pay attention to his wife so that he can act.

PT: His wife was there when he was acting?

BD: Of course. And when I want him to say something about love, I only talk to him about his wife, Brigitte, telling him to think about Brigitte, "Emmanuel, think of Brigitte!" And he gives me his shine, he give me his pain, but thinking about Brigitte. The audience does not know about that… For me, an actor is like filming a tree… It's true. I need the truth people can give, their truth. So if I choose an actor, he is the one I film. I have to maintain contact with him. I do not care about his training. If I choose him, he has to be human. So I do not care if he is an actor or a mason. I have met many an actor who has asked me, *"What should I do?"* And I felt that they were empty, yes, that's right, in need of a character. Which I understand, but I do not have any answers for them.

PT: What disturbs me in your work is its capacity to slide into the temporality of each actor-being, what Julian Beck called the "actressor". You give each of them the time to develop, whereas most often the director controls the length of a scene. In my opinion, this unique work on the intimate time of your actors is what distinguishes your films from other contemporary filmmakers.

BD: I know that I want to disappear to the extent that what I like is developing the character. And what drives that is the time of their development, not mine. It is certainly not the display of my virtuosity. My art is what takes places in front of me, and I am of absolutely no importance, I watch. The time is the actor's time. The time of his or her development. To achieve that, no one moves, the camera moves very little, it submits. I think there is a necessary submission to what you film.

PT: But the camera does not disappear… It remains very present all the same.

BD: Yes, but as soon as someone tells me that the shots are very elaborate, that they are well framed, it upsets me. I would prefer that no one think about it, otherwise it is an error. If the shot is too composed, it doesn't work. You have to eliminate it. There is the work needed to eliminate totally the making of the film, the director and the rest of the team, to bring out the subject itself. You must disappear.

PT: Being present in this disappearance...

BD: Totally.

PT: To obtain presence, the reality of the actor and no longer narrative reality. I think this is the way to approach the question of reality along with the notion of documentary that was bothering you before. Precisely in the real time of the beings and things you come into contact with and that you release from the constraints of the screenplay.

BD: Yes.

PT: Which explains the feeling some might have that your films are like documentaries. But in that case the time of beings has chance distributing the events and not the opposite.

BD: That comes from the appearance of the time of life, the monotony of reality and duration. We are in real times. Time that is stretched out, the true time of the scene and that, simultaneously, leads us into fiction. The viewers enter the imaginary. That is how the imaginary comes about and it's contradictory because everything is real. When people treat my work like documentaries, when they say, "He makes documentaries," they are wrong. Even if I understand their mistake.

PT: If it isn't a documentary, isn't it still a document concerning an interiority?

BD: Yes, even when I'm filming outside, I am only filming the inside. The film itself is the interior, from start to finish. That is why when I film a landscape, it is the character's interiority.

PT: Are you more of temporal than a spatial filmmaker?

BD: Yes, of course. When I was with Freddy, we were inside him. The empty streets, that is him. The entire decor is the expression of the character's interior state. You cannot film the invisible. You can only film visible things, but I know that by continuing to film the visible, all of a sudden, you pass to the other side. You have to wait, like an ascetic. You have to wait and it will necessarily shift, it's obvious. Something happens. It does not even depend on me. But I see it in the shot, it becomes something else, and in time. Time causes it to happen, not acting, not words. It's the duration that causes the shift into something else, precisely this unknown world—which is the interior world, the self, a mystery—and that art tries to express through all its various possible forms of expression. But reality in itself does not interest me, only the emotion of reality is worthwhile.

PT: This shift into interiority is due to time, that is true, but also due to what is unfamiliar to the actors, to fact that they do not know...

BD: It is tied to unconsciousness, to innocence… Rossellini said the same thing about his actors, "They do not need to understand." I have no need for knowledge; it is not a question of knowledge or clairvoyance, not at all. There is something else. Cinema is not connected to those things, cinema involves emotion. The body of each spectator must be modified. And the body is modified through time, through its duration. By what else? There is the exposure time of the audience, in other words, when I think the viewer is sufficiently exposed, like in photography, "That's enough, cut!" That is all editing is for me, the exposure time of the audience. That is all I want them to understand… They get hit and then it's gentle. The whole film is built like that, on relationships between opposites. The violence comes from this contact between opposites. Between boredom when nothing happens… and then, all at once, the din of the scooters. All art, Chaplin said, presupposes an understanding of human nature. The members of the audience have a body, have sensations, have time. In all these shots, what do they look at, what do they see? A spectator in a movie theater, it's extraordinary, we play with him the whole time. The film is not important. What is important is what happens to the spectator and what happens to him. So it is better to abandon any pretentiousness or stylistic vanity of the type "I make films to express and explain!" Absolutely not.

PT: And the emptiness?

BD: Emptiness may be the condition necessary for the audience to change. Violence, cruelty, roughness are also regressions, a return to something primary to alter the sophistication in which we live today. That is why I choose rustic people. And my characters are so expressive because they are all unfinished. They are expressive in contact with the bodies and minds of the audience because the audience completes them. I must be drawn to this roughness. It is the shapeless matter placed in front of the spectator's face.

PT: What do you say to people who see you as a Christian filmmaker?

BD: They are making a mistake. I am trying to be a filmmaker. Period. We are confusing the spiritual and the sacred. I am not Christian. I am above all someone in doubt. I despise the religious, the clerical. I think that there is something profound in human beings, something mysterious, bound to the sacred. The sacred is also in the profane, when there is something else that takes it out of the profane, and the camera is capable of showing it because it is something we experience ourselves. It appears to me. That is why a landscape is no longer a landscape, it resonates with me. Why? Because I make it resonate, otherwise it doesn't say anything, it remains silent. But if I am sad, it is sad; if I am happy, it is happy. It's an endless process. I work with creatures, objects, subjects, people, each of us imperfect but in search of our own perfection. There is no cinema of reality. You need unreality, which is its substance.

PT: What then are the arguments of those who identify you as a social and political filmmaker?

BD: They were related to subjects like racism, the integration of North Africans in France, the National Front extreme right party. Some people even said I was a conservative filmmaker.

PT: *That's really strange.*

BD: Yes, it came from…

PT: *What?*

BD: The fact that a bastard becomes the hero.

PT: *In* The Life of Jesus?

BD: Exactly.

PT: *Freddy, the one who kills the North African? But he is not a hero. Only a profoundly racist reading could say that.*

BD: I agree. The problem is always who is watching. I have heard everything and its opposite. Making these sorts of films, you have to expect it. Some spectators are also bastards.

PT: *There is also this alternation that I brought up at the beginning of the interview between a calm and collected sensuality and its aggravation into a certain bestiality.*

BD: This position is closest to nature and therefore to the instincts. Showing civilized human beings, in a movie theater in the 20th-21st century, their nature. Showing complete people holds no interest for me. That is why my characters are incomplete. They do not need to be finished. They are not concepts or spokespeople. They are half-human, if you prefer. We do not need a model. People ask me, "*Have you ever seen anyone make love like that?*" No, but who cares! I deal in representations. I prefer taking that particular aspect from sexuality, filming it alone and bringing something partial, unfinished to the knowledge of the audience. I do not need to have an exhaustive response to the question. That said, in *Humanity*, for the position of the body of the young girl, the vagina, the blood, etc., I did ask a forensic scientist if it was accurate. I have a need for verisimilitude but one that stops very quickly at the level of appearance.

PT: *Isn't it the need for truth, more than precision, that gives your work its political dimension?*

BD: Why political? I know I need its truth.

PT: *Isn't it this need, this demand for truth that is profoundly political?*

BD: I do not understand why you are talking about politics.

PT: *I am not talking about politics but about the political, the concern for humanity in human government.*

BD: Yes, maybe… But a cinema that moves towards beings and lets them develop in shots, in durations, and not a vain cinema that concentrates on the "me" with actors as its elements, no. I will say it again: I do not think cinema is a type of knowledge, political or otherwise.

PT: I am not talking about knowledge or about skill in the backrooms of power, but about participating in the collective reflection on what makes men disciplined brutes, who perform wicked deeds with a clean conscience.

BD: Yes, maybe… What I am saying here comes from my experience. Because a glance, a movement, a silence have captivated me, I try to adjust them rather than reproducing a textual support. Otherwise, it does not work for me.

PT: That is what I find to be profoundly political, these movements to other levels of conscience that a glance, a gesture can produce when removed from the constraints of so-called social dialogue.

BD: Yes, but it is a question of the interpreter. And here, there is not even an interpreter. When you say interpret, he interprets something else.

PT: He doesn't stand between what he has to say and what the text would say in his place.

BD: Exactly! Something that come from above and for which he would serve as a voice, well, in this case, it's the opposite. There are no more voices, everything is focused on the actors.

PT: For me, what you look for with them, what you ask them to become in this duration makes you political. In the same way, aren't you also in a Christ-like dimension, in the sense of the primitive Christ? The happy Christ, happy to have become incarnate in man instead of the Christ painfully displayed on the cross by the Catholic religion.

BD: I think truth lies in existence. There is a desire to take the Christ and make that film, to disincarnate or make incarnate in another way. But not to go back to the origins of Christianity that are in the Word, wouldn't you agree, the spoken Word… But *The Life of Jesus* is not the Word. On the contrary, it is the body.

PT: When you are shooting your films, do you do many takes?

BD: Not many. Each morning, the actors know, for example, that it's the scene in which the two cops go visit the father. They know that but nothing more. They do not know what they should say. I watch, I watch what is going on. While the crew is getting into place, I have them act out the scene once, quickly, loosely, and I say to myself, "that's good." There is no excess work, because then the work becomes intellectual, reflective, which is horrible.

PT: A risk of psychologizing, of justifying its limits.

BD: Precisely. No psychology and as few explanations as possible, nothing is said. All of a sudden, there is very little talking.

PT: But in a language that is like a foreign language inside the French language. In The Life of Jesus, *it is the "chti-mi" dialect of Northeastern France, and the English subtitles on the tape I saw really helped me.*

56 ▶

BD: The sound engineer kept telling me, "*It's hard to understand what they are saying.*" I asked him, "Is it a problem with the sound levels?" "*No, it's an articulation problem.*" Well, too bad, because if I ask him to articulate more, he will articulate and be false. I think each being has a truth, you have to ask each of them to be true. That is all and then they are true.

PT: So they should become foreign to what they been made to become.

BD: The fact that the actors are in a fictional work is terribly important. And no one can help that. There is a scene that is there and to a certain extent, I do not have very much to do. There is a scene written where the character goes down the street on his scooter and then falls down. In any case, he is going to fall and that's that. There is something written and, during the filming, it eliminates the work with the actor that I cannot stand. I stay in the background, watching from afar, I do not get too close.

PT: In this same line of thinking, in Humanity, *the scene of the kiss in the police station does not follow what is written in the screenplay.*

BD: That is also the difference between what you can say, what you can write, but that you cannot film. There are things that cannot be filmed. I think cinema comes before literature, that it returns to the writer's material itself. When I write a screenplay, I want to put feeling into the words. I think that with cinema, I can go directly to these feelings. At least I can… I try to capture life itself in the end, in other words the material used by a writer. So when I am filming, I do not shoot the screenplay, I do not film what is written. What is written is a way of memorizing the substance that I want to approach. I remember writing, for example, "she cries, pregnant with the crime." You cannot film that and there are plenty of things that I have written of the same nature that are impossible to film. At the same time, when I write, I don't worry about writing things that cannot be filmed, that is not important. What is important is possessing a certain energy and the power of cinema is to come before literature and precisely to return to something primitive. What is it? It is life, it is time. We are within time, and therefore in a physical relationship and, if they want to, the members of the audience can choose.

PT: Those are what I call thought shots, these sorts of static shots, the active immobility of thought.

BD: That's why when I say that the moment of writing is a moment of intellectual thought but cinema does not follow that. Cinema has to regress in comparison with writing, it has to return to the origin.

PT: Words no longer form a screen between individual and thing.

BD: Yes, my screenplay explains things but it is cumbersome.

PT: But the texts are beautiful.

BD: Because you have to go all the way with writing just like you have to go all the way with cinema and cinema is not, absolutely not the end of literature. It is more

 59

complicated... It is not spoken, but it is also poetry. That is what they have in common. Thought is a landscape... it is Marie and Freddy on the chair lift then falling on the plowed fields... It is a travelling shot like that one, everything is there. It is a thought-shot.

PT: But it is also expressed by body movements, a language of corporal movements that resonate with the poetics of space in which they develop.

BD: Yes, they are often silent glances. They are contemplative shots. The worst thing would be having them say what they think. That would lead to a redundancy and a risk of obscurity. No shots then, when they mean what they think they say. That is why my repudiation of dialogues is logical in relation to power of shots and the soundtrack that remove the need for words. So words add nothing and perhaps, they even bog things down and prevent them from occurring. The dialogues are purely functional—"I'm going there, I'm doing that"—and never contemplative. The contemplation either lies in the meaning or in the shot, but not at all in the words. In the project for *The end*, it's the same, the dialogues are really banal... None of them mean anything, signify anything or are contemplative.

PT: How does the story line, the narrative come about since there is no desire to signify especially using facts?

BD: It comes first of all from a search for banality. The story line should not be strong from the start. It involves a search for a lack of force: no force in the actors, no force in the decors, no force in the dialogues, no force in the shots. In the end, when you add all that together, it makes up a lot of little forces that become a force. A major force like the force of an absolutely gigantic plot? No. The plots are banal and are never exhausted. I think there is a balance... That is why I like neutral things, neutral acting, neutral decors, mostly neutral plots and something will necessarily happen when they end up interacting. And the audience is not neutral. They are able to take part so that meaning emerges. When people ask me about the story and what I meant to say, I reply, "Nothing..." There has to be a story because the time must move on. I like police stories because it is a good movement, with someone who is searching, so there is some suspense... But once I have set the plot in motion, I deal with other things.

PT: I would like to discuss with you the question of the angle of takes, the position of the camera, to the extent that it always establishes a point of view, taking sides for or against starting things or events. According to what you say, the position of the camera is a pretext. What happens to a scene based on this pretext?

BD: I know that in any determination of a point of view, of camera location, the center is the place of choice. In other words, being at one with what I film and not being a point of view, forgetting that there is a camera that will be set up and that will serve as an axis, on the contrary. I know it does not mean anything to eliminate the point of view, but I still try to do it anyway. It is a useful utopia.

PT: The point of view of the watchful "I"?

BD: The "I" does not count. No, what counts is what I am filming. But you need a point of view. There is no point in being naive. You cannot put the camera everywhere. There are no absolutes and I do not think there is a dominant place that is best for the camera. You need to decide that the camera is going to be there and want to put it in a certain place. For example, I do not cover, filming like this… and then like that… taking care of it during the editing. I do not want to have a choice. I have done it in video. You end up with forty shots and no idea which one to choose. So it is necessary to impose a point of view even if there is no absolute point of view, even if there is no true point of view. The only truth is that I film relatively. You necessarily have to stand somewhere, so I place myself there. Why? It depends. Why not? It can be a purely practical element, a movement that means a certain spot is better than another. Next, I cut my scenes simply because I do not want to be dependant on the shooting. I want to be able to modify the things I film so I have to cut. I cut a number of my scenes with wide and mid-range points of view and surfaces. There are always three, four values in the shot, no more. There are practically no continuous motion shots because those are the types of shots on which I no longer have any grip. And then the actors are movie actors, people that have to be cut. They are not theater actors, you cannot let them go on for two hours, it's not possible, they cannot do it. So you have to stay near them, and that is what cinema is, staying near them. I told you, I have to fight with the make-up artist to keep her from adding anything. Everyone wants to add something. There is a crew and the crew has to be motivated by what it is doing and to do it successfully. When we watch the rushes and say, *"that is some fine work,"* but there is nothing, no technical virtuosity. It is rather flat. I film in a rather flat way without trying to move around, to move the camera. I do not see how that helps. If I do a zoom, it is because something is about to happen that I think calls for it. But I only move when my actors move, otherwise not at all. I always stick to them. The point of view is a unification, always eliminating my subjectivity. As soon as I feel that the framer is preparing a sophisticated composition, I change the frame. But he wants to do it, he is a photographer. I move the camera to avoid entering the aesthetic domain. I am afraid of beauty.

PT: But do you make your film while shooting or while editing?

BD: During each instant that leads up to the editing. I am often shocked by the mediocrity of the things I film. When I shoot Emmanuel on his wall as he looks around, nothing happens. There is some noise, people go by. In the editing room, something happens. You might want to say, "Something needs to happen here, it needs some action!" Well, no, nothing happens and if it is neutral, I know something else can happen during the editing. So I do not need a spectacle and I realized that with *Humanity*. It is hard on the technicians, I can tell, they get bored, it takes forever. I can feel the lethargy

60 ▶

61 ▶

of the technical crew, the electricians, the machine operators, because not much happens and there is not much light. I often see them leave the screening room surprised with what they have seen. The editing does that. The actors are also surprised. Filming is virtual, the substance. The worst thing would be to stop at that point.

PT: As a filmmaker, not being afraid when filming, seeing that nothing is happening and letting it happen takes a certain amount of calm…

BD: Yes. You cannot be afraid of incompleteness. Cinema works with time. Its means of production are slow and you have to be patient. I like this work, waiting but with the knowledge of the power of each moment and their limits. That is why directing is an asceticism. When I organize my crew, I pick people who would come to the films I make. The same as with the actors, I do castings with the technicians. Some of them disappear during the shooting because they cannot handle it. With *Humanity*, I had a number of problems with a set designer who could not stand the fact that I did not want to change anything and who left because he had trouble dealing with it all.

PT: I think you have also said that you do not like to add any artificial lighting…

BD: I choose the most natural light exposure, and, there again, no lighting points of view. In *Humanity*, the lighting always came from above, it is diffuse and there are no points of view. The lighting does not highlight anything. Lights are needed because we have to be able to see well enough, but that is all. Light lets you see but says nothing. You can also play with the choice of colors. For example, I wanted an image that was denser but that did not say the same thing as the dramatic content. On the contrary, it could not have been all black because then it would have been sad. However, I need artistic elements that use contraries, even in an actor's performance, in an expression; or an ironic soundtrack for certain situations, like a police car that is having trouble getting started even though we are in the midst of a drama. But precisely in this case, I think it is necessary to add a second or even fourth degree of meaning.

PT: But there, it was an accident?

BD: Yes, but during the mixing, I can do what I want. There, I chose the accident. Emmanuel walking along and catching his foot on a manhole cover, I took that too. We could have done it again, but I felt it was there. There were also many places in the film where his voice changes, you can feel that he is not well, but I took it. I make all those choices on the day of shooting. Waiting for accidents… And I know that the film can be found there. Putting everything into place while waiting for what will happen and wanting what comes. It's a stoic attitude.

PT: Your images are very pictorial, the relationship between colors, frames where the positions of bodies and decors are very studied.

BD: I spend a great deal of time… I do not arrive on the set out of the blue. I have already gone out alone for days on end scouting the terrain, wondering how I am going to film it. And I don't know how, but I do it. I don't have ideas right away, but by being there, always coming back to a place, I take my paper and begin to sketch out scenes. And the day I arrive on the set, I know what I want. That is how I work because I am not spontaneous and a crew needs quick answers. I spend a lot of time with the cameraman discussing the image. In other words, breaking him. Everyone who works with you is someone with his or her own desires. They have to be broken down, to be harmonized with the film, by taking away their desires so that each of them becomes a part of the film. It takes time.

PT: When you work with your cameraman, do you refer to particular paintings, certain atmospheres?

BD: That is how I begin, but right away, I try to connect him with something that exists, since, in order to talk to him about something that does not exist, I have to put him in contact with something concrete. I lead him towards pictorial or other references to explain tones or colors, certain browns, for example. Next, I take him out into the field and explain how I am going to film. Then I have him do some test shots and look at what he does. If it doesn't work, I don't take him. What takes a long time, actually, is the work of convincing people to make a film in which they have to submit. They all have different tendencies. You have to understand them. It's like an actor who has an idea, knowing if it is a good one or not. You have to know what you want.

PT: There is a constant and fascinating alternation throughout your films in the editing between landscapes that open spaces of meditation and the emptiness of cities.

BD: Yes, it takes me forever to find neutral backgrounds.

PT: I noticed that there was the same relationship between the landscape and city shots in Humanity *as at the end of* The Life of Jesus *between Freddy and the passing cloud…*

BD: That is what is so extraordinary about filming things that are so neutral. No one would pick the street in which *Humanity* takes place, there is nothing there. The hardest part is choosing that street because spontaneously one would pick a street that held some meaning. That is a mistake. The decor is a neutral element. It should not have much meaning at all.

PT: It is borderline fake, unreal, almost a studio set… like a decor in the natural decor.

BD: That is not far from the truth, like when we chose the backdrop of a farm in disorder. That is important, because we spontaneously go to the beautiful, the orderly, the significant and I know that I have to get away from all that. My decor has to be neutralized in a certain way, so that it is not too significant from the start. I think filming a beautiful landscape is foolish. It has to be in harmony with the character, which comes out in the editing by associating his or her glance with a shot. The shot cannot be too meaningful.

The shot of Freddy at the end is just a simple shot and its force comes from the editing. I think that all cinema is an art of editing, that meaning comes from the editing and therefore less from the filming. The fear I often have to say, "I'm not filming anything," well, I weather it quite well. From time to time, the technical crew looks at me thinking that I am going to say it is no good! Everything happens according to my convictions. I am the one who decides it is great when no one else has seen anything and they think nothing has happened… that the actor will have to start over. Actually, no. You shouldn't finish a shot during filming because it is an element and it has to keep its provisional and relative status as an element. It should be completed during the editing, in other words in association with another shot. During the shooting, you have to make shots worthwhile, reduce them, be patient.

PT: In The Life of Jesus *and* Humanity, *there are contemplative scenes, shots that are waiting for a humanity to appear… Is that right?*

BD: I am a person who waits. I wait for the audience to act, not so much the actor. The actor does not complete the work, especially because that is the worst that could happen; so the actor should remain silent long enough, stay reserved. There is an actor's reserve that seems to be to be the contrary of what we see today with actors who want to put everything on the screen. The person who should be finishing on screen is the audience member, which supposes a certain humility, moderation, reserve. This reserve is what makes the film something tenuous, moderate, where the audience can find a place, since if everything is there, it's already over. It is also an enigma, perhaps, something unfinished, incomplete.

PT: In Humanity *and* The Life of Jesus, *there is no answer to the quest. We remain in the incompleteness of the question.*

BD: When someone asks me, *"What is the answer?"* I reply, "I don't know… I am not the one to ask, I am just an intermediary." That is why—and this is political—I take the audience to be the end, the goal. And the audience counts, not in terms of a concession because concession is not the point, but in terms of an awakening. Cinema is an awakening. I am not convinced that today's consumers are awake, but they need to be woken up. To wake them up, we have to start from where they are currently. And not to keep them in one place, on the contrary.

PT: This awakening you mention, what you call establishing contact with the audience in an easier way by using their current language whereas their attention is always interrupted by other attractions as in the walkman generation, don't you find it illusory? Let me use an image: don't you think someone is more awakened by one of René Char's aphorisms than by the hit single playing on the alarm clock radio every morning?

BD: No. I showed *Night and Fog* by Alain Resnais to students, and I heard some of them laughing. They laugh because there is something they don't get, that doesn't get

through. And I think that the problem is not Resnais, the film is not the problem for them. The problem is that what they are watching is inadequate, they need to be awakened but not necessarily by the intelligence of what they are shown. You can show them the most beautiful paintings in the world, they will probably be over their heads, at least they might be… So the problem of the awakening is to start with them. They are the ones who have to recognize the importance of what they are watching. It is better for them to watch something basic that awakens them than to show them the seventh wonder of the world that, in any case, will not awaken them. You have to be humble and abandon certain pretensions and certain high-placed views. René Char's poems might be over their heads, which would be a failure. Something fails with them; it fails with some people if not with you.

PT: From experience, and I don't agree with you because I have been a teacher, I think that you can awaken with René Char or difficult poets like Jean-Pierre Duprey, Ghérasim Luca in suburbs that everyone else has abandoned simply by reminding these disenfranchised listeners that with these poets, they can take back a vision of humanity from which they have been voluntarily excluded in the name of their so-called class inaccessibility, their cultural isolation.

BD: It is a pedagogical question. Even if I say something very intelligent and they do not understand me?

PT: It is not a question of understanding.

BD: And what if they are not awakened to that? The most important thing is to start with them and pedagogy might just be accepting say simpler things that they understand and that make sense to them. I quickly got out of secondary education to teach young people in technical schools, people who were more concrete intellectually. The awakening can take place starting with a course on the performance and capacity of a milling machine instead of quoting Antigone. You have to know the people you are talking to. It is important to stimulate them, and if you have to talk to them about things they like, such as computers, etc., then so be it! That does not mean talking about computers or something they expect… You have to lead them on, take them somewhere else. It is only a means of expression. The milling machine will end up expressing something other than itself, it's obvious.

PT: But starting from them, as you say, is not what interests them, because what interests them is what they have been given to keep them from finding themselves, their base… this departure from themselves.

BD: They master what they understand. If they prefer rap, well, there is also good rap with poetic forms in the words. We cannot give up and say that the truth lies in Char's poetry. There is surely some truth there, but you have to have a more daring mindset and say that there are truths to create with the means and the forms of communication we have today. You also have to renew your choices and not always believe that the truths can be found in Apollinaire, Baudelaire, Char, etc. That is not true. Young people need modernity and when I say modernity, I also think that there is an alienation from modernity. I think there is a very strong contemporary alienation but that the only way to get out of it is to awaken people at the level of their own sensibility. If you play Bach for them all day long, they cannot do anything with it and, in any case, they won't listen to you. What should you do? That is the problem for television and the cinema today and the solution is not to continue doing things that they do not want to understand, that they cannot understand. The problem is to lead them to get out of there. But to get them out, you cannot do it directly because there are people today living in economic and social situations that must be dealt with first. For me, it is a political problem and not an artistic one. There is a political revolution that needs to be engaged before tackling the question of starting to read poems by René Char.

PT: I do not share your distinction of priorities or the necessity of a revolution prior to learning about Char. I think it is all contemporary and that it is the separation, the division that is the ideological hindrance to any movement towards awakening or emancipation.

BD: I showed *The Life of Jesus* in the Parisian suburbs and many people were not even watching the film. It was a real mess. They couldn't stand the time, the length, etc.

PT: That is not a problem. The rupture is more important.

BD: They didn't give a damn. *"We don't want to see this,"* is what they told me. I know where they are from too.

PT: But there they are caught up in the production of the fantastic, the illusory.

BD: I doubt that showing this type of film every evening at 8: 30 would change anything. Let me go back to what I was saying earlier, about having a didactic project, I think that there is education and that education is first of all political, in other words, it is in the political choices we make ourselves in the organization of society. As long as society remains organized the way it is, it's over. They won't change.

PT: Very pessimistic of you.

BD: The only possibility is a political change. And I believe in politics. I think that a single political revolution is capable of modifying the conditions of existence and life for a majority of people and that by modifying these conditions of life, we can change their sensibilities, their view of the world. The question I ask myself today is what should be done to create this passage. And I don't think that is by putting all the beauties of the world in their face that they will change. I don't believe so. I would like to, but I don't. So, we have to try to express something that touches them, that says the same thing, but that stimulates them. We should not abandon that search. The conversation between the two is what is important and not me in front of them or the contrary. It does not mean saying that you are like this so here is something you will enjoy, which is what modern marketing does and that is why it is so dull and so stupid. That is why I was talking to you about my third film, *The end*, and I will not be the first to throw in the towel.

PT: *Are you going to make them throw in the towel?*

BD: If I can take a step forward, so can they. They have to take that step, otherwise it won't work. It is not a pedagogical film; I just look at where they are, watch what they are doing and try to ensure that they do not systematically leave slamming the door shut behind them.

PT: *Your third film is entitled* The end. *The end of what?*

BD: *The end* is the end of a certain type of cinema… their cinema, their films with their actors. It also shows the end, the deterioration, the decadence of a certain American universe that serves as a model, and I think that the natural relationship one should have with films is not a relationship to a model. Revolutions should happen in the streets, not in the movie theater. Cinema should be left in its place.

PT: *But it can participate in the revolution…*

BD: There is little risk that cinema would take part in a revolution today since it is pure entertainment. People go to the movies to take a break, not for what I call an awakening. In my opinion, cinema, on the contrary, can open people's eyes, but it is only an ingredient. The only person who can start a revolution is someone in the street.

PT: *But what is the street today? We walk along the street without leaving it, subversively speaking. Maybe there is a need to go into theaters to see something else and then take to the streets again. There was a period in cinematic history when films were considered to be political instruments. The Cineccita was built under Mussolini for propaganda purposes, the Soviet Union built vast studios…*

BD: But current cinema is entrepreneurial, reflecting our consumer society. It does little more serves as a major element of the dominant American culture that disseminates its economy, its consumerism through its films. Look at how the people are dressed! American cinema provides models for lifestyles, clothing and thought. It's cultural imperialism. And it works, really well. It is an ideological and political instrument and a catastrophe.

PT: *It is a means of colonization.*

BD: Yes.

PT: *That you hope to penetrate?*

BD: Yes, by reversing it. Because, as I was saying earlier, if people do not come to see the films there is a problem… a problem of efficiency. You have to go where the spectators are.

PT: At the risk of being had.

BD: Of course, but which option is better? Staying in your corner without taking a risk, talking about truth, filming it… intimately… or on the contrary taking risks.

PT: How do you think your directing is influenced by the implications you spoke of earlier concerning the content of your work?

BD: This is important because a filmmaker's writing is his or her directing. The way the person decides to set the camera, to choose an angle, frame, length or space. For me, that is the most interesting question you can ask a filmmaker and not the question of meaning. Meaning is a subsidiary question. Directing is a question of finding an expressive language. And if that language is expressive, it must have meaning, it must awaken the spectator and bring something edifying to him or her. So the questions I ask myself today are often directing questions. In other words, how to approach a scene with the complexity it contains, such as the decor, space, time, text, actor, etc. There is a complex of events that have to be made to coincide and that have to create harmonious music. At the same time, it has to work for the contemporary spectator's ears as well. For example, the choice I am now making to say, "I am going to use this kind of professional actors." This is a director's choice, a choice of expression. By saying, here is a body, a physique, an appearance. Then there is the directing that takes shape through the narrative, the story I am telling and all the decisions I make. The choice of colors, of movements, of situations that I deliberately choose as conventional situations because that type of cinema is made up of conventional situations, that's all you see. And I do so precisely to take them apart, to distort them, but I can only distort something I have exposed. I have to expose it first. *Humanity*, to a certain extent, distorts from the start, it does not expose. The choices made are quite radical. I chose to deform the inspector from the start, but he is deformed, already deforming. Whereas if I take an actor, I have who is recognizable and whom I can deform… whom I deform in time, making him do things that disturb the spectators, but in order to disturb the spectators, they have to be there.

PT: You mentioned the inspector in Humanity, *but the commissioner on the other hand is not deformed.*

BD: He is less deformed.

PT: Does that allow the confrontation between the two, does it make it clearer and increase the spectator's surprise between here and there, next to each other? How do you approach it? Is it something clear in your methodology?

BD: Yes because you need a center that appears real with characters who are completely real. In *Humanity*, the mother, Joseph are not deformed. Only one of the characters is a bit dissonant. But he is on the edge. And if all the other characters had

66 ▶

been like that too, it would has been a decline. No one would have understood the film. It's just like an instrument that is not tuned. And Pharaon was like that, even more so because the film was completely the opposite, real. The perception of this dissonance also comes from the rest.

PT: Do you set yourself a dogma for each film?

BD: Yes, I look for something, I have principles, I have a set of images… I have a lot of elements that I try to tie together through a dogma. But each film has its dogma. This time, I change the color. I am not dogmatic. There is a search for truth, sincerity, things for which I cannot compromise, things I would never do. And at the same time, I don't know what they are; I only know there are things that I can't do… I would like to stop doing the same thing, for example looking at *The end* again and saying "oh yes, it's the same thing!"

PT: In any case, a filmmaker, any artist has a style even if he or she deals with different subjects.

BD: But the person's style should be able to reach out to other things. All the art of directing is facing that. So I prefer moving around, going to other countries. A director puts things in order. Here, I put things in order while filming in California. I have the same spatial and temporal problems but the landscapes change, the language as well. So much the better, my style is a putting into order, in my own way. The actors are not the same, but my work is to tie it all together and that is what defines my directing. I think my directing is not ideological but it is formal to a certain extent. Maybe if I went to Japan, I would want to make a Japanese film.

PT: Don't you have a number of other films in mind, even some projects that are already well advanced?

BD: Yes, I have other film projects, including an American film, *Twenty nine Palms*, that I would like to finish rather quickly. But I do not want to film all the time, to do one film after the other, the investment is too great and I have a great desire to work. I need to scout out locations, to see for myself… that takes time. For example, I am going to film in the desert and to find camera angles in the desert, you have to go looking for them! It takes a long time because I have to understand the location. And then, because I do not delegate the scouting to my assistants. I look for the decors myself and when I go looking for them, I try to find a harmony that is not easy to locate. In this film, I have many shots to do downtown so I went to Los Angeles but I didn't understand the city. So I am still incapable of putting a camera anywhere, and as long as I haven't understood, I won't be able to do so. Seasides and deserts I can handle, but I have trouble with cities. Since I film quickly and do not do many takes, the result of this preparation is that I know what I want. I arrive each morning, put my camera in place, do a test and it's in the bag. There are no more questions, about how I should film… Everything has already been done. I mostly talk with the actors without rehearsing, so I need to work, to be sure of what I am doing. At the same time, it's terrible, I don't trust anyone.

68 ▶

DIALOGUE IN SPACE AND TIME

VALÉRIE JOUVE: *As a photographer, I am interested in discussing with you what you call your means of expression and, first of all, the distinction you make between a shot (plan) and an image.*

BRUNO DUMONT: The difference is that I work with a crew and so I do not hold the camera. Even if there is always the desire to reduce the size of the crew. There is something heavy-handed in the very notion of the shot. The term in French (plan) is used in architecture, in economics, and presupposes a certain order. It is also a martial term, an aggressive term. While image is much gentler.

VJ: For me, image and shot cannot be distinguished. When I talk about images, I am not thinking about visual media but rather a particular form of thought inherent in the image.

BD: An image is more objective and a shot more subjective. The word "shot" has something in that involves the will.

VJ: The term "photographie", as it is typically used, refers to the English word "picture". However, the word "image" also exists in English and includes a nuance that does not exist in French. The two words are quite different. I think that this difference might concern the notion of duration. In "picture" there is the idea of taking an instant, of stopping time, while an "image" connects ideas that are concentrated together in a fixed space where thought develops in a different way than in language. So when I speak of images, as a photographer, I mean "image".

BD: When I make an image, it means I have failed. That what I've done is immobile. Taking a shot, in the language of cinema, is a moment; and therefore in time.

VJ: I am now working with still images, but maybe this notion changes as soon as you change equipment. I realized when writing the screenplay for the film I am now preparing that the things I imagined as a photographer when starting to write changed depending on the means of expression I have been trying to put into place for the cinema. In photography, you cannot escape the still image, and that might be why I try to juxtapose different shots in a single image that work on different times.

BD: In my case, I know that I am trying to escape that more and more, to look for what I think is the sign of cinematography: the relationships between shots. In other words, neutralizing the shot as much as possible, emptying it and precisely looking for the agreements that favor something in the duration as it is; not in the image.

VJ: But you use images. In Humanity, there are times when everything stops, and it is no longer just a still shot but a still image.

BD: Yet for it to stop, it has to move. Otherwise it cannot stop. I look for a rhythm in order to break it. Like having an airplane pass overhead in order to hear the silence that follows. You really need noise to hear it, otherwise silence cannot be perceived even if there is silence.

VJ: In photography, this question is related to formats, and it takes shape in space through different scales that make it so that everything stops all of a sudden or accelerates the rhythm of the eyes, playing with temporal differences... And then playing with the differences in temporality...

BD: Yes, everything is a break.

VJ: Like in the scene where the police car breaks down just as it is about to drive off, the door opens and an airplane passes. The image stops. It settles and allows the eyes to set on it, on a meaning even if it is produced without the desire to hold it.

BD: There might be times when it slows down so much that I end up becoming visible, but I think that is a mistake.

VJ: How can you work without those moments?

BD: I admit that I have difficulty with photography to the extent that I do not understand it. First of all, it is a silent art.

VJ: Silent, maybe, but one that plays here with acoustics in its relationship to space, not in relationship to sound.

BD: It is an art that is very hard to read.

VJ: It is very slow. That is why there is such an enormous difficulty with photography today—which is also the difficulty with a certain type of cinema—and its relationship to consumption.

BD: I would add that I understand photography when I see a series of an artist's pictures, but not just a single picture.

VJ: I agree, and understand you better.

BD: In photography, I understand the relationship between photos. For example in your pictures what I find attractive without really knowing why are the very wide angle shots, especially the photo The Authors that has a great deal of mystery in its title.

VJ: In this image, the question of the fake is brought to the fore. I worked on it as an ironical take on the belief that has developed around the image. An association of ideas that cannot take place over a duration of time but that can evoke an image in terms of volume, rhythms and the dialog between them all. And that continues in the exhibit in the arrangement of the images in relationship to each other.

BD: How can photography be done today taking into account the fact that we have television, cinema?

VJ: It is not the same at all. Taking photographs today means moving about, being in a different temporality.

BD: But where is the time? When I edit a film, I create the time of what I am doing.

VJ: You make time, but it is also determined by the time of the 24 frames/second.

BD: Yes, there is a visible, audible duration to which I submit.

VJ: But in an image, the time of the viewer creates the duration. This time develops the photograph differently. Passing time fills the image and heightens its presence.

BD: The time comes from the viewer like in painting. The time I spend looking at a photograph.

VJ: And positioning myself to look at it.

BD: It's an enormous risk.

VJ: Yes, but it is interesting to play back that time. When I decide to exhibit these photos on a white wall, the white wall becomes as important as the image. The image does not stop at itself and also calls on everything that surrounds it.

BD: This type of off-camera area does not exist in the same way in cinema. During a film, everything is black. And the audience focuses on the screen. With photography, there are the surroundings, the wall, sounds, people… A photograph projected in a movie theater would produce a different idea of time for the audience than in an exhibit.

VJ: That sort of experiment, producing meaning depending on the exhibition spaces, is something that interests me a lot, the relationship to space, to the body of viewers.

BD: But photos preexist the space in which they are to be hung.

VJ: Each image was made very independently from an idea that set it in motion. But depending on the exhibit space, there are images that I choose and others that I would not show because they would not be appropriate.

BD: That's editing.

VJ: In this editing, the image also has a different time.

BD: The editing associates images, lengths of time.

VJ: But what do you mean by shots?

BD: Shots are the way cinema captures the image. It is on the one hand a drawing in space, I isolate the on-screen and off-screen, I choose and therefore eliminate, I set the frame. Then there is the duration, then the movement inside the frame, the soundtrack and finally the audience. Expression in cinema includes all of these things.

VJ: These elements are specific to cinema. In photography, this notion of shot would be to return a duration to each image through the successive shots that compose it. A way of constructing the image, a flattening that leads from one shot to another.

BD: Yes, the shot has surfaces. In cinema we call that shot values. You associate shot values: wide to close values, or close to close…

VJ: But there, we're talking about distances, about the focal length used.

BD: There is the focal length, there is also the film exposure; you can correct it with filters. The recording or more precisely the developing establishes the relationship between cinema and photography. It is true, you have the frame, the values. What is particular to cinema is movement.

VJ: For example, in Humanity, Pharaon has a very specific type of movement when he rides a bike and fills the frame. In that shot you find strongly emphasized body movements that bring me back to the notion of the fake. Does the recording of this movement take place because of the means of cinema? Or is it simply the recording of real movement?

BD: No. Capturing reality is seldom possible. Pharaon is here on the side on a fake bike pedaling with a speed damper. His position is not real but true. At the same time, I cannot take him too far. I like the fake and its disposition. There is a machinery, so it cannot be true. Here, you cannot imagine that he is riding a bike with the camera following him. Well, because it is fake, let's work on it and try to catch the truth. The truth is not found in an exact reconstitution of reality, but probably in its alteration. For example in the acting.

VJ: But in relationship to the fake, I think that you and I take different positions because we do not work with the same equipment. I basically cheat with the spatial relationships. If I want a face to face encounter between two people on two sidewalks, and if I am working with photographic equipment, the distance between the bodies, the scale translated by the photographic equipment does not work for me because it does not correspond to the emotional perspective. Editing allows me to rework and recreate what I saw in the scene and that simple photographic recording does not provide. Whereas in your films, the distance from reality is essentially found in movement. It is true that I am bound to translating this subjectivity through an image while you transmit it through a series of images that create movement. Thus I often noticed the falsifications in time shifts and accentuated movements. But there is also the need to construct connections with different worlds for your characters, like these off-camera situations with the presence of the landscape.

BD:… Mental landscapes. It is a question of shots, it is only mental, it is no longer reality. The only element of reality in cinema is the audience. You can take the greatest risks with them because they can be there. So all the art of photography or of cinema can be found in this conversation. And the decisive moments are in the appearance of the audience. I am increasingly trying make films that include this important place for the audience. They form a body, a voice, an ear. What is cut short is the attempt to captivate them, to seduce them. That is why it is important today to understand their cultural and intellectual development, to understand their sensibility, because they have to understand what we show them. Take popular films for example, they are always very short, fast, with high levels of tension and always spectacular. This means putting the audience into such a physical state that, when they are caught, they cannot escape.

VJ: Your cinema does not abandon this idea of working on the audience including direct sounds, the quality of voices.

BD: It is direct.

VJ: Yes, but at certain moments, you might think that the acoustic space of the voice is not the same as the space of the image. And then you hear the sound of a key in the lock that establishes the connection with the place.

BD: You can have dissonant acoustics to give relief. But the fake starts at the beginning of the film. When in *Humanity* you see a small character walking in the distance and you hear his breathing in the foreground when you should be hearing small birds because he has a lapel mike. In reality, you are already inside the character.

VJ: The danger would be to think that it is naturalism. In the end, the displacements you operate through time slips, sounds, lengths of time all question our point of view. When you mention means of expression, is there one that you prefer for best reaching the audience?

BD: First of all, being in their desire is what counts.

VJ: In other words, everything that is put in play by the mechanisms of transformation, selection, priority.

BD: Cinema, like photography, is a means of expression. It is a means, which signifies understanding all the possibilities offered by the language of cinema: camera, photography, directing the actors, sounds, movements through space, intonation, pitch…

VJ: Which means that thought relies on the object.

BD:… So, using all these means to achieve my goal, the point I am hoping to reach. A means of expression expresses something on the level of a human truth. When Matisse was asked "What is painting?", he replied, "Well, take this table, for example. I do not paint this table literally, but the emotion it produces in me." A means of expression is a way to express what existence lets me experience in the world in which we live. We have a view of the world, and making a film, taking a photo means bringing that perspective, rendering, giving through the means of cinema.

VJ: Whence the difficulty in saying which means would be the most important since everything is in fact interconnected.

BD: That is why I say I do not like photography because I do not know where its place is. I work with a director of photography because I am not a photographer and do not master the tool with all its problems, the apertures, etc.

VJ: As a photographer, all of those elements are means of expression. What is different is that we have a still image and it is necessary to concentrate, to fix an entire experience in an image.

BD: But it is only one moment.

VJ: Yes, but the moment can be charged.

BD: In my films, the problem is not whether the photography is beautiful or successful. The problem is what happens inside. I also want it to be more and more neutral, so that it is unassuming, that it stays in its place…

VJ: That's the filmmaker talking, but I do not think that what is called photography in cinema is the same thing as the work done by a photographer.

BD:… Because I have to combine photography, directing the actors, the acoustic space, the duration… all of those aspects. A film is a complex whole.

VJ: Photography is a passage. The moment of the frozen image combines with others and develops an attitude over time. The machine only allows you to take one instant but the image is also dependent on the way you use the machine. Does a filmmaker have to take the camera at any point?

BD: I need to have the frame, to make it.

VJ: You also have different frames for bodies. All the distances are there and at the same time, it is always changing position before continuing. In this film, what I call still images, which are not the same as still shots for me, are certain moments when there is a need to pose. Not as a way to sum up, because they are not connected to the plot, but all of a sudden this time is taken to measure up with space. This measurement accompanies and restores a position to the characters and the audience that is not the protagonist's position. It questions the posing. It does not show the figure as a hero. It is displaced. In any case, it is as powerful as the protagonist but it does not involve that relationship at all.

BD: What you are saying is no doubt related to the fact that the characters talk very little and to what is emphasized by this refusal. To say that we will listen to what they will say. Since that cannot take place at those moments, the eyes are fixed, not on what is missing, but what is there. The body necessarily emerges in this refusal to put into words and these neutral decors since we stay with it.

VJ: The reduced body movements as well.

BD: Maybe this time spent not moving is related to photography. What I like about CinemaScope is that it is difficult to be mental. The most cerebral format is the square format where you can capture what you are thinking. With the Scope, you necessarily "pick up" a little on each side. It is a format that I had trouble assimilating the first times I tried it. I could not get the shots the way I had thought of them, they didn't fit. But the fact that it picks up like that on either side has been good for me since it eliminated me. It kept me from sticking to my motif by letting me seek out happenstance.

70

71

VJ: Your shots of places—in particular what you did in the suburbs: brick walls, landscapes, interiors… or in the street—are often more evocative of American photography—I am thinking of Eggleston—than American cinema for example.

BD: Wouldn't that be more a question of the format from the CinemaScope?

VJ: Eggleston's format has nothing to do with CinemaScope. And then in Humanity, *this format is in the entire film, whereas it is only in the relationship to the street in particular that I felt it. I do not think it is the format of the frame but rather the nature of the bodies. Your characters are "ordinary" people but they assert, in their reduced movements, real postures in this street framed in a very wide angle.*

BD: But that is also very ordinary. The Scope has the ability to transform banality. The motif has to be modest in order to let the shot have all its power. My work as a filmmaker is to find incomplete backdrops that correspond mentally. They must be restrained enough to be able to develop an exchange with the camera, with the frame. Like the actors' faces: they are not too beautiful or too ugly in order to be beautiful or ugly at certain moments of the film. I am increasingly looking for neutrality. So I have to choose a material that is not too dense to be able to associate something neutral + something neutral + something neutral… And hope that the language of cinema, which is the synthesis of all that, gives it force. A force that is not only visible at a given moment.

VJ: The force of your films also relies on the image—I do not know how to say it otherwise—where the body is related to the camera. In each image, the body truly gives the measure of the frame. When you say force, I think that in Humanity *power plays a significant role in the difference between these levels.*

BD: True, bodies produce the movement in this story. The camera is always as close as possible to these bodies. The landscapes do not move. The bodies move. And if there is a panoramic shot, it means the bodies are in motion.

VJ: There are moments in Humanity *that touch me deeply. The time, for example, when Pharaon turns on the television without the sound then plays his player piano and starts to sing. That moment has an emotion that is not there, however, to produce an emotion. And that happens all the time in the film. It is just there without needing to support its meaning. It really corresponds to a sensation of what it is to exist. At certain points, it drifts and at others it is solidly anchored. The two states meet and are never separated. This effect does not only rely on musicality, sounds… It is the combination of all the images, the sounds… the train that goes by with Pharaon's silent but very loud cry. I also wanted to evoke this effect in one of my images, Josette, the desire to call on sound in an image. A passage, a length of time reminded me of that particular image.*

BD: There is also the influence of the detail on the whole. The details have to be combined together.

VJ: For example, in Humanity, *are the three bathers on the beach characters you worked with just because they were there?*

BD: No, they were in the script. It is always in the script. However, when shooting, I do not try to provide an exact illustration so much as provoke what is written. I am looking for something else. For example, to avoid freezing the three bathers in an exact reproduction of what I wrote.

VJ: About the notion of the actor, would you agree with statements made by Rossellini who also worked with non-professional actors and who said that a reeducation took place in front of the camera?

BD: Yes, we take care of that in the first hour! The most important question in this debate is the director: the choices he or she makes. The actors do what they can. You have to respect what they can to do and understand that what they can do is what I want. For example, their voices are their voices! I don't want to change that. Why they change from time to time, I don't know. They also have intonations, movements… I want their substance.

VJ: A character produces the difference.

BD: In fact, it's having a character like that and seeing him in relationship to others. The fake engenders the fake. He sounds fake to the ear but then you adjust yourself to him. An professional actor would have been discordant.

VJ: Is this difference a strategy for captivating the audience—strategies in the sense of an idea in the shot with the military reference that you mentioned earlier in your different conceptions of the shot?

BD: Yes. It's like with the roll of film: the time of impression. I often talk about the exposure time of the audience. I cut when I think the audience has had enough exposure time. To sense something, you need time. And if the bodies in my films are slow, it is because you have to enter into them. The audience has to be impressed. The manufacturing of the atmosphere starts there.

VJ: As a result, the difference in this character has an effect on everyone. But when you are thrown off-track you become available for things again. It means losing a familiar territory…

BD: Yes, he is different, but he has his own truth. I had to keep it because his truth was the only thing he could bring with him. Most of all he cannot be ridiculous or ridiculed. I have to be sure that he is correct, in his own accuracy, his truth.

VJ: What are you looking for in your audience?

BD: Their presence, their eyes, their angle… so that they complete what they have in front of them. I am looking for their "feeling".

VJ: The audience is the outside world, real people.

BD: Today, unfortunately, we count the number of entries, not exits. You cannot make films or photographs against people, it is impossible.

VJ: That means bringing questions to where things are happening, even if these questions will no longer be important ten years from now. At a certain point, you want to accompany these questions—which are not necessary political—while being here now, and how.

BD: First of all, you have to know what you want this art to be. A photo has to awaken me, bring me something as a human being. People who go to the movies leave and then live their lives. Something has to happen. And that is the question, perhaps: getting along better with one's self, finally. That is surely a step forward.

VJ: The audience is the other self?

BD: Yes, the audience responds. I only exist in the eyes of others. It's obvious.

VJ: Starting to speak also means entering the public sphere: you are allowed to speak. It is not so much whether your words are pleasing or not, but that different types of words create a balance. And when you take a picture, or make a film, you give certain words importance.

BD: A work of art has to recognize the audience. When they look at a photo they should recognize themselves, the photo should speak to them and place them in a position of equality and balance. It is even a democratic relationship. We have to move beyond the old aristocratic relationship to stars where we watch television and films like poor people. Cinema has to establish a healthy relationship, where the audience is worth as much as the film they are watching because they also make the film. When I say that I will reduce the thickness of the film as much as possible, it is in order to leave them a place. You have to be with your times, contemporary.

VJ: Today, the question of temporality seems essential. Quick time is only interesting if there are slow times.

BD: In this sense, photography has a rather weak fiction quotient in relationship to films and I think you can speak the truth through fiction. Photography brings me something, it informs me, but I do not feel it has the power of cinema.

VJ: But fiction can mask things or at least be used to mask. Fiction for me is something that can lead you far away from truth. By the way, what kind of truth do you think you can reach through fiction?

BD: Precisely the certainty that truth is not in reality but in the perception of reality. That the world can only be seen through me, that the horrors I see on television leave me cold because there is no room left for fiction. Because fiction is me, in other words, the capability of returning a sensibility to what I see.

VJ: But does that necessarily have to pass through a story?

BD: I think so, because we are in History, we are in time. Stories are often more important than History because by telling stories—and there are oral traditions that reach back to the dawn of time—we give meaning to History better than when reading History books. I think we need the story. Stories are vectors. The audience enters them.

VJ: And poetry?

BD: Poetry is necessary because it is the flesh and blood, but the story is the skeleton.

VJ: Now I understand better the idea of a viewer who changes status and becomes an actor.

BD: The audience has incorporated modern cinema. They see films today differently than they did before. Their sensibility has changed. Today, they are film consumers.

VJ: But wanting to touch the audience, even if there are contemporary ingredients, is not enough. There are certain ways of operating.

BD: I do not want to touch them but establish a connection with them. Not being different, not excluding them. People have to come. It's true that films are made today to get people to come, but I do not want that.

VJ: Have them come so that a dialogue is established.

BD: Yes, so we can talk.

VJ: Like wanting to see someone. So with the idea of a meeting.

BD: Yes, so that an encounter takes place. For example when you talk to French people about American cinema today there is a desire.

VJ: With images, there are also stories; encounters with people, events and therefore History like you have with the actors. So, how do you work with this dialogue, ensuring that there is an encounter with people who interest you?

BD: The most important thing is being satisfied with what you do, being just. The place of the audience, in any case, is not a question of numbers but with having my films find their place in the era in which they are produced. That's all. Doing cinema simply means making a film. It does not mean asking what cinema is. The place of cinema has changed. Thirty years ago, there were film lovers with an artistic cinematic culture. Today we have mass consumers looking for distraction. It's a political and social problem above all. Cinema is just following suit…

VJ: You make films because you love cinema, not because you want to talk about it. I can also sense this pleasure in making films very strongly in the play of differences between images and sounds.

BD: Yes, there is an irony in the sound in relationship to the images. Sound is the most interesting part of cinema.

VJ: If sound is more important than the image, do you privilege sound over the image when you seek out the rhythm of shots?

BD: Everything is related. The shot, the sound, the rhythm… The time of the sound or of the shot.

VJ: Then how can the sound be the most important part?

BD: I think that the emotion always comes in the end from the sound in a shot and the tie between them. I can dub; I can keep the most satisfying image, get the sound from another take and dub it over. If you watch closely, you can notice a lot of minor problems with labials, a good deal of minute problems that you do not see. Then the "true" often appears, in that way.

VJ: I wonder how you can make a conversation real with a camera, a team, just like that in real time.

BD: Only the set-up that you construct makes it possible. One part is trust. Otherwise everything works against the conversation. Action! "Action!" is a harsh word. In any case, everyone has to agree. There is a given moment when you have to ask for silence in order for things to begin. So, there is only the set-up.

VJ: But it is rather cumbersome.

BD: You get there layer by layer. You do a take but you might have made a mistake, so you do another. You have this choice. You can cut and not say that you are making a continuous motion shot and hope that everything goes well like in the theater. When I get home after a day of filming, I always have the feeling that what I have done is mediocre, and it often is second-rate. But once these things are edited together, their status and therefore their worth change.

VJ: You said that you work on the images in your films at the locations you pick out yourself. Do you also write the dialogues while scouting?

BD: Yes. I have already seen most of the scenes that are written. They are imitations. I am afraid of writing an artificial scene. I do not give the screenplay to the actors because they would feel like they are reciting a text. That is why I talked about a set-up. You have to improvise and at the same time say what is written.

VJ: In the film I am preparing, I wanted to have a meeting between characters with whom I had worked individually. I figured that the sound recording would not necessarily take place when we were filming, that there would be too many people for a real dialogue.

BD: Get them some drinks!

VJ: Really?

BD: You cannot start out by wanting things that are too difficult because they won't work. Desire little at first and you can accomplish what you want to do. For example, while filming, eliminate text first. Why? Because it is no good. I cut… I cut. Most important of all is getting rid of things, being accurate. Knowing how to get rid of scenes that you filmed because they are no good. You learn how to make a film by making films.

VJ: It is very strange for a photographer to move into duration. When you write your screenplays, after writing a first version, do you work on it again to break its linearity?

BD: No. I know that writing is one thing, filming is another. Writing simply helps define a story line that puts me into a certain state. But when I film, I have to take full advantage of what happens between the predictable and the unpredictable.

VJ: Yes, but in writing the screenplay itself, do you impose narrative rules on yourself?
BD: Probably.

VJ: Don't you want to break the chronology?

BD: I have no problems with chronology. But with dialogues, it is a different story and since I do not like to write them, I note the intentions. Otherwise, natural chronology works for me. I prefer natural appearances. Having everything seem unassuming, avoiding abstract, artificial things.

VJ: But when you say you do not want artificial things, your character Pharaon is artificial when he rides the bike. That must not be the problem since it is not because it is artificial that it is not correct.

BD: I would say that I need a certain aspect of appearances. After that I avoid reality because I like deformation. But it cannot be heavy-handed.

VJ: With a feeling of truth…

BD:… Without leaving verisimilitude behind. The fake aspects come in fact from the shooting. You cannot film a guy on a bike "just like that", it's impossible. Moreover, the car makes noise and you cannot record the sound. You then have to dub the scene and his voice would not be the same as at that point. So you create the poetry, you have something that is distorted. That is what cinema is. What is extraordinary are all the possibilities of the language of cinema. And to make films, you have to know these possibilities and then desire them. There is the image, but there is also the sound, there is the actor, the camera movements, horizontal, vertical… There is a complex web of things and, to make a film, you have to understand that at the very least, in other words submit to it, resign yourself to it. It is a difficult art because it exists over a length of time. Making a good scene is easy but here you have two hours and you have to go the distance. Hardest of all are short films because they are a short exercise in which you have to create a duration, an atmosphere. It is not easy. With feature-length films, you can use natural time because they are long enough. You don't have to say anything in the end. Just show a little bit of our existence, a little bit of atmosphere.

BIOGRAPHY

Born in March 1958 in Bailleul (Nord), he studied philosophy at Lille and Paris, and taught for a while in Lille. There, in the same time, he realised his first film commissions for industry, famous brands, banks...

Currently he is preparing Twenty nine Palms and The end which are planned to be shot in the United States in the coming months.

FILMOGRAPHY

Around 40 short films: documentaries, advertising and institutional films.

Short fiction film:

1993 PARIS (PARIS)
(15', 16mm colour)

Feature film screenwriter and director:

1996 LIFE OF JESUS
(90', 35 mm scope colour)

Cast:
David Douche (Freddy)
Marjorie Cottreel (Marie)
Geneviève Cottreel (Yvette)
Kadder Chaatouf (Kadder)
Sébastien Delbaere (Gégé)
Sébastien Bailleul (Quinquin)
Samuel Boidin (Michou)
Steve Smagghe (Robert)

Screenplay & director: Bruno Dumont
Executive producers: Jean Brehat, Rachid Bouchareb
General administrator: Muriel Merlin
Director of Photography: Philippe Van Leeuw
Sound: Eric Rophe, Matthieu Imbert, Olivier de Nesles
Sets: Frédéric Suchet
Music: Richard Cuvillier
Make-up: Férouz Zaafour
Costumes: Nathalie Raoul, Isabelle Sanchez
Editors: Guy Lecorne, Yves Deschamps

Sound editor: Pierre Choukroun
Mix: Thierry Sabatier

A 3B production/ CRRAV/ Norfilms co-production, with the participation of the PROCIREP/ GAN FONDATION / National Centre of Cinematography/ Ministry of Culture / CANAL +

Awards:

Fondation Gan Prize,1996
Special Mention Caméra d'Or at the Cannes Film Festival, 1997
Critics Prize for FIPRESCI at Chicago Film Festival, 1997
Sutherland Trophy for Best First Fiction work, London Film Festival, 1997
Jean Vigo Prize,1997
César Prize, 1998, nomination for the Best First Fiction work
Fassbinder Prize at the European Film Awards, Berlin 1997
Actors Prize awarded to David Douche at the Taormina Festival (Sicily),1997
Shooting Prize at the Avignon Festival,1997
Palmier d'Or at the "Mostra de Valence", 1997
Best Film International Critics Award at the Sao Paolo Festival, 1997
Michel Simon Prize awarded to M. Cottreel at the "Acteurs à l'Ecran" Festival, 1998
Best first film, best screenplay et best supporting role for K. Chaatouf at the Festival d'Alexandrie, 1998
Arsenals Prize at the Riga Festival,1998

1999 L'HUMANITÉ
(148', 35 mm scope colour)
Officially selected for the Cannes Fim Festival, 1999

Cast:

Emmanuel Schotté (Pharaon De Winter)
Séverine Caneele (Domino)
Philippe Tullier (Joseph
Ghislain Ghesquière (Police chief)
Ginette Allègre (Eliane)

Screenplay & director: Bruno Dumont
Executive producers: Jean Bréhat, Rachid Bouchareb
General administrator: Muriel Merlin
Director of Photography: Yves Cape
Assistant directors: Xavier Christiaens, Claude Debonnet
Production manager: Nicolas Picard
Sets: Marc-Philippe Guerig
Costumes: Nathalie Raoul
Make-up: Férouz Zaafour
Sound: Pierre Mertens
Editor: Guy Lecorne
Sound editor: Mathilde Muyard
Mix: Jean-Pierre Laforce
Original music: Richard Cuvillier
Music: Pancrace Royer
Pièce de Clavecin by William Christie ©Harmonia Mundi

A 3B Production
Co-production: ARTE/ France CINEMA/ CRRAV
With the participation of the
National Centre of Cinematography
CANAL+
PROCIREP and the Jean Vigo prize
With the help of the Nord/Pas-de-Calais Region

Awards:

Prize of the Jury and prize for the best Actor and Actress at the Cannes Film Festival, 1999

PHOTO INDEX

1 to 6 Desert/California

7 to 10 Desert/ Views across Los Angeles

11 to 15 Joy-Stevens house/Malibu/California

16 Police Building/ L.A.

17/18 Desert

19/20 Loft/ L.A

21/22 Streets/ L.A

23 Joy-Stevens house/Malibu

24 Downtown/ L.A

25/26 Mansion/ Hollywood, L.A

27/28 Desert

29 to 34 Big house in Pasadena

35 to 40 Mansion/ Hollywood, L.A.

41 Beach/ L.A

42/43 Turbines. Desert

44 to 46 Desert

47 to 49 Loft/ L.A

50/51 Mansion/ Hollywood, L.A.

52 Apartment/ L.A

53/54 Desert

55 to 63 Hotel/ L.A

64 Loft/ L.A

65 to 69 Desert

70 Cemetery

71 à 73 Surroundings, runway Military base, California

also available from Dis Voir — website http://www.disvoir.com

literature/fine art/cinema

Bruno Dumont
- *Life of Jesus*
- *Humanity*

Raúl Ruiz
- Poetics of Cinema
- The Book of Disappearances
  & The Book of Tractations
- A la Poursuite de l'Ile au Trésor

Peter Greenaway
- The Falls
- Rosa
- Fear of Drowning by Numbers
- Papers – (Paintings, Collages and Drawings)
- The Cook, the Thief, his Wife and her Lover
- The Baby of Mâcon
- The Pillow Book
- ZOO
- The Belly of an Architect
- Drowning by Numbers
- Eight and a half Women

Manoel de Oliveira
- Angelica
- Lisbonne Culturelle
- Les Cannibales

cinema

PLASTIC ARTS

Paul Ardenne, Pascal Beausse,
Laurent Goumarre
- Contemporary Practices (art as expérience)

Michel Gaillot, Jean-Luc Nancy,
Michel Maffesoli
- Techno (an artistic and political laboratory of the présent)

François Dagognet
- In Favour of Today's Art

Jean-Yves Bosseur
- Sound and the Visual Arts

Thierry de Duve
- Clement Greenberg between the lines

Alain Charre, Marie-Paule MacDonald,
Marc Perelman
- Dan Graham

Gertrud Koch, Luc Lang,
Jean-Philippe Antoine
- Gerhard Richter

Christine Savinel, Jacques Roubaud,
Bernard Noël
- Roman Opalka

Christine Macel, Marc Perelman,
Jacinto Lageira
- Jean-Marc Bustamante

Jeff Wall, Ludger Gerdes, Hervé Vanel,
Ingrid Schaffner
- Stephan Balkenhol

Jean-Pierre Rehm, Olivier Joyard,
Danièle Rivière
- Tsai Ming-liang

Jean-Marc Lalanne, Ackbar Abbas,
David Martinez, Jimmy Ngai
- Wong Kar-wai

Paul Virilio, Carole Desbarats,
Jacinto Lageira, Danièle Rivière
- Atom Egoyan

Michael Nyman, Daniel Caux,
Michel Field, Florence de Mèredieu,
Philippe Pilard
- Peter Greenaway

Christine Buci-Glucksmann,
Fabrice Revault d'Allonnes
- Raoul Ruiz

Yann Lardeau, Jacques Parsi,
Philippe Tancelin
- Manoel de Oliveira

Éditions Dis Voir: 3, rue Beautreillis – F-75004 Paris
phone (33 – 1) 48 87 07 09 – fax (33 – 1) 48 87 07 14
email: disvoir@aol.com   website: http://www.disvoir.com